SATANIC PANIC

A MODERN MYTH

By

Rosie Waterhouse

Copyright © 2023
ROSIE WATERHOUSE
SATANIC PANIC
A MODERN MYTH
All rights reserved.

No part of this publication may be reproduced, distributed, or transmitted in any form or by any means, including photocopying, recording, or other electronic or mechanical methods, without the prior written permission of the author, except in the case of brief quotations embodied in critical reviews and certain other non-commercial uses permitted by copyright law.

ROSIE WATERHOUSE
Printed Worldwide
First Printing 2023
First Edition 2023

The Author asserts her moral right to be identified as the author of this work.

DEDICATIONS

To my father Jack Waterhouse, an inspirational creative character, architect, pianist, composer, who set me off on the journalism trail, because, he said, I was good at English and very, very nosey.

To Phillip Knightley, my journalistic hero and friend, who encouraged me always to keep digging.

To Harold Evans who inspired me with the pursuit of truth-seeking investigative journalism.

And to my beautiful mother Sheila Waterhouse, who just wanted me to be happy.

With thanks to dad who sent me the Serenity Prayer when I first left home:

God,
grant me the
Serenity to accept the things I cannot change,
Courage to change the things I can, and
Wisdom to know the difference.

Credited to American Theologian, Reinhold Niebuhr (1892-1971).

PREFACE

I never intended to publish my PhD thesis as a mainstream book. It's an academic work, a piece of history, perhaps of interest to a few scholars I thought, on a very niche topic, which I and a few others called, the 'Satanic Panic'.

At the time of writing, it's coming up to the tenth anniversary of the limited publication of the thesis, in four bound copies and on City, University of London's library website in January 2014. And a lot has happened since then to change my mind.

What used to be a rather obscure and esoteric but to me fascinating fringe topic – a belief in so-called Satanic Ritual Abuse – has taken off as a global conspiracy theory, amplified and spread through social media.

Extremist proponents of the theory claim the world is run by an elite international network of paedophile Satanists who rape and sacrifice babies and children, drink their blood and eat their flesh. Practitioners are supposed to include senior royals, celebrities, politicians, judges, journalists, police and the military; in fact virtually anyone who could be considered Establishment.

Believers in the conspiracy are particularly active in the USA and the UK, where I have been following their antics since 1990, when I first began investigating the origins and spread of the 'Satanic Panic' for the UK newspaper I was then employed by, the *Independent on Sunday*.

After five months of digging I concluded that despite hundreds of police investigations, in particular in the USA and later the UK, during the 1980s, there was no physical, forensic, conclusive, corroborating, evidence that Satanic Ritual Abuse existed. The memorable headline in the *Independent on Sunday* of 12 August 1990 was "The Making of a Satanic Myth".

What I did discover was clear evidence of the origins and spread of the myth. In that era - the 1980s - before widespread use of the internet and social media, belief was spread chiefly by Evangelical Christians, social workers, adult psychotherapists and "anti-cult cops" in books, seminars and on the international conference circuit.

In 1994 a UK government commissioned inquiry which examined the evidence in 84 alleged cases of Satanic Ritual Abuse in the UK from police, social services, the NSPCC, the Official Solicitor and family courts reached the same conclusion. The official report concluded there was no evidence of Satanic abuse as defined - whereby sexual abuse was a ritual directed to worship the Devil and part of a Satanist belief system - but found three cases where trappings of rituals were used to frighten children into submission and silence.

I firmly believe no conclusive evidence of a Satanic ritual sex abuse conspiracy exists to this day. Over the years people taking an active interest in the Satanic Panic have occupied two polarised camps – believers and sceptics. It will be clear I am in the latter. I justify my stance, as an objective investigative journalist, reinforced by the ethos of one of my PhD supervisors, Chris French, now Emeritus Professor and Head of the Anomalistic Psychology Research Unit at Goldsmiths, University of London, that to be a true sceptic, one has to be prepared to believe with evidence. I am and I stand by that.

After completion and limited publication of the PhD thesis in January 2014 I focused on my full-time job as a senior lecturer and Director of the MA in Investigative Journalism, a course I developed and ran at City, University of London.

I continued to keep an eye on a few key zealots promoting belief in the existence of Satanic Ritual Abuse and to research allied controversies, such as the fierce debate, in the fields of psychology, psychiatry and psychotherapy, over recovered versus false memories, and the validity of the diagnosis of Multiple Personality Disorder, latterly re-named Dissociative

Identity Disorder. These supposed afflictions were said to be a consequence of extreme childhood trauma such as sexual abuse, including, so believers claimed, Satanic Ritual Abuse.

I published a few freelance articles, mainly in Private Eye magazine. Little did I realise my niche Mastermind topic was about to re-surface as a conspiracy theory and very soon go viral worldwide.

A bizarre phenomenon called Pizzagate suddenly emerged in the USA in late 2016, morphed into the QAnon movement in 2017, and together they have since attracted millions of believers worldwide. There is not the space here to delve too deeply into the detail and it's outside the scope and timescale of the PhD but I'll give a very brief precis. And I'll try to explain how Pizzagate and QAnon are an extension and expansion of the Satanic Panic.

A few weeks before the US presidential elections held in November 2016 the mischievous Wikileaks hacking enterprise released leaked emails obtained from John Podesta, the then Democratic candidate Hillary Clinton's campaign chairman.

Looking for any damaging material about Clinton and her camp, Trump supporters and conspiracy theorists interpreted some content as coded messages about child trafficking and paedophilia. They latched on to conversations about pizza and

Italian food and homed in on a particular pizza parlour in Washington frequented by Democrats.

A wild false rumour – with the Twitter hashtag #PizzaGate - spread that Clinton and her top aides were involved in the sexual abuse and trafficking of children, with Satanic overtones, in the basement of this pizza parlour. The tales were soon elaborated to include ritual murders and the drinking of blood. The problem with this scenario was this restaurant has no basement.

Pizzagate was very soon convincingly debunked by numerous investigations by various police departments and several highly reputable mainstream media outlets, notably the New York Times's "Dissecting the #PizzaGate Conspiracy Theories" of 10 December 2016.

But that did not convince or stop the conspiracy theorists; if anything it reinforced their belief that 'The Establishment' were involved and conspiring to conceal it. This illogic helped establish, entrench and spread the even more extreme extension and expansion of the Pizzagate theory to the QAnon movement, perhaps most notorious for its involvement in the storming of the US Capitol Building on 6 January 2021.

QAnon has its roots in Pizzagate and before that the Satanic Panic. It first emerged in the USA in late 2017 but soon spread globally, again online, through social media and the alternative universe of the 'dark web', a secretive hang out for deluded and some of them dangerous deviants. Its origins are in the American far right.

At time of writing, the identity of Q is unknown. But originally, allegedly, Q is or was an anonymous (hence QAnon) White House insider who originated and spread fabricated claims of the existence of a cabal of elite international paedophile Satanists whose horrific activities include the trafficking, torture, rape, sacrifice and murder of babies and children, cannibalism and the "harvesting" of their blood to extract a mythical substance called 'Adrenochrome' which apparently serves as an 'elixir' of life. In the alternative cultish world of QAnon, Donald Trump is the hero out to expose and defeat these dastardly devil worshipping villains.

Why are Pizzagate and QAnon relevant to my PhD and subsequent publications on the Satanic Panic, given that they occurred after completion of the PhD in January 2014? Because these have become allied conspiracy theories; they reinforce and amplify each other. The zealots are themselves like a cult – secretive, obsessive and paranoid with a belief that a corrupt "Establishment" conspire to cover up Satanic Ritual Abuse.

So what is the format of my PhD thesis, or dissertation, in this small book, and why am I publishing it now? It's called a PhD by Prior Publication, whereby my published and broadcast journalism on my specialist subject, over many years, is the body of work, and I had to relate that journalism to the academic literature in four fields: the psychology of memory; the anomalistic psychology of weird beliefs; the sociology of moral panics; and the theory and practice of investigative journalism. In 20,000 words. The literature is vast and it took me two years. After the viva the examiners asked for more detail. I eventually got permission to write 32,000 words, plus references and appendices. I call it a PhD lite. A truly scientific PhD of uniquely original discovery can take around seven years and 100,000 words.

Nevertheless, I do believe my published and broadcast journalism, and my critical analysis of it, do make a contribution to knowledge, as the rules of the PhD process require. I recently decided it was worth publishing in the mainstream, for any interested reader. And I also wanted to inform law enforcers, lawyers, judges, child care and mental health professionals, politicians, the media and public opinion-formers who may encounter claims of Satanic Ritual Abuse and urge them to ask themselves, "what's the evidence"?

My next book will include a collection of some of my published stories, since the PhD of 2014, plus new material about some weird, shocking and deeply worrying events in this bizarre episode in history, up to date.

Satanic abuse, false memories, weird beliefs and moral panics

Anatomy of a 24-year investigation

ROSALIND THERESA WATERHOUSE

A thesis submitted in fulfilment
of the requirements for the degree
of Doctor of Philosophy:
A critical analysis offered for
the PhD by prior publication

At
City University London
Department of Journalism

January 2014

VOLUME I: DISSERTATION

Contents

Acknowledgements 15

Declaration 17

Abstract 19

Part 1 – Introduction, contribution to knowledge and summary 21

    Introduction 21

    Contribution to knowledge 30

    Purpose of this PhD 34

Part 2 – A summary of the origins and spread of the Satanic panic and some chief 'claims-makers' 37

    Satanic ritual abuse: definitions. 37

    False memories and multiple personalities 38

    Satan arrives on the scene 44

    International spread 53

Part 3 – My investigations into the myth 61

    How it happened 61

    Methodology and conduct of research 70

        ➢ Methodology 70

        ➢ Conduct of research 76

        ➢ Investigating 'The Making of a Satanic Myth' 81

Part 4 – Theoretical interpretations 89

How my work relates to the theory and practice of investigative journalism 89

- ➤ The role of other journalists in the Satanic panic........ 89
- ➤ What is investigative reporting?................ 92
- ➤ Method 98

How my work relates to the academic literature in the field of psychology on false memories and multiple personalities . 101

- ➤ The 'memory wars' 101
- ➤ Research reviews: false memory 104
- ➤ Recovered memories, multiple personalities, alien abductions and Satanic abuse. 108

How my work relates to the academic literature in anomalistic psychology (the study of weird beliefs) 112

How my work relates to the academic literature on moral panics 122

- ➤ Definitions................ 122
- ➤ Models of moral panic theory 124
- ➤ Satanic ritual abuse and moral panic 126
- ➤ Aftermath 131

Part 5 – Analysis of data evidence or outcomes 135

Part 6 – Critical appraisal of previous work 145

Responses to my work................ 145

Conclusion................ 147

References 149

Appendix 1: Critical appraisals **170**

a. Jean La Fontaine 170

b. Mike Hill... 172

Appendix 2: Citations of published journalism............ 176

a. Articles 176

b. Books 177

Appendix 3: List of published and broadcast journalism submitted as my body of published work 180

a. Published articles.. 180

b. Television.. 188

BBC *Newsnight* 188

BBC1 *Real Story* 189

c. Radio 189

d. Film 189

e. Book chapter 189

f. Conference talks 189

g. Presentations.. 190

h. Professional memberships 190

Acknowledgements

To my supervisors Michael Bromley and Chris French for invaluable guidance and support.

To Jean La Fontaine for her friendship and wisdom over 20 years.

To Mike Hill in New Zealand for sharing his encyclopaedic collection of papers and being my mentor.

To Sarah Churchwell for seeing the potential of my proposal.

To Christie Slade and Howard Tumber for encouragement and support. To Peter Ayton for guidance and approving a budget for books. To George Brock for supporting my sabbatical.

To Jacqui Farrants for her enthusiasm and sharing her review of research on false memories, which gave me a head start.

To Linda Lewis for providing such efficient sabbatical cover and to Melanie McFadyean for constant friendship and support.

To Martin Conway for his encouragement and guidance.

To Paul Anderson for a brilliant edit.

To Lis Howell for brow beating me into embarking on a PhD.

To Peter Wilby for fostering journalism to 'find things out'.

To Stephen Glover for publishing 'The Making of a Satanic Myth', which got me started.

To Anna McKane for encouraging me to pursue the teaching of investigative journalism.

In memory of my mother, father and aunt Tess who encouraged me to achieve my potential.

Declaration

I grant powers of discretion to the University Librarian to allow this thesis to be copied in whole or in part without further reference to me. This permission covers only single copies made for study purposes, subject to normal conditions of acknowledgement.

Abstract

This critical analysis focuses on my investigations over the past almost 24 years into what I term the 'Satanic ritual abuse myth' – or 'Satanic panic' – the controversy over recovered versus false memories, and, more recently, the validity of the diagnosis of multiple personality disorder (MPD), now known as dissociative identity disorder (DID). This reflective analysis, written for the PhD by prior publication, explores how my journalism has made an original and significant contribution to knowledge in my own field, investigative journalism, and how it relates to – and has contributed to - the literature in several academic disciplines – the psychology of false memories, the anomalistic psychology of weird beliefs, and the sociology of moral panics. I was one of the first researchers internationally to conclude there was no physical, forensic evidence that Satanic abuse existed. My 'Making of a Satanic Myth' feature, published in the *Independent on Sunday* in 1990, has been cited in the literature, along with key investigations since. I describe the methodology and conduct of research during my continuing investigations into the origins and spread of the 'Satanic panic' and related controversies of false memories and multiple personalities. The dissertation itself adds significantly to academic theories and historical accounts of these events from the 1980s until today. Through a wide reading of the literature I have pieced together a forensic chronology which provides a unique overview of a particular era of striking and peculiar phenomena. On reflection, I conclude that my investigations provide evidence for the concept of moral panics created through an 'explosive amplification' of anecdote, social and official concern about issues such as child abuse, spread by 'claims-makers' and a globalised mass media. Although sporadic claims of Satanic abuse continue I conclude there is still no corroborating evidence.

PART 1

Introduction, contribution to knowledge and summary

Introduction

This dissertation focuses on my investigations over the past almost 24 years (at time of submission) into what I term the 'Satanic ritual abuse myth' – or 'Satanic panic' – the controversy over recovered versus false memories, and, most recently, the validity of the diagnosis of multiple personality disorder (MPD), now known as dissociative identity disorder (DID).

The dissertation begins by outlining in brief how my publications have made an original and significant contribution to knowledge and to my particular discipline – investigative journalism – and then relates my journalism to the academic literature in the wider fields of research in the study of recovered and false memories, weird beliefs, and moral panics. I am submitting with it a list of publications and original broadcast material which constitute a coherent body of published work.

My investigations demonstrate how journalism can intersect with several academic disciplines and clinical fields – from the psychology of false memories and weird beliefs to the sociology of moral panics. I argue that my journalism has made a significant contribution to the stock of human knowledge about the bizarre outbreaks of claims, internationally, of Satanic abuse, the interlinked recovered memory movement and, latterly, the controversial diagnosis of multiple personality disorder.

My investigations have been conducted according to a long-established tradition of fact-finding, evidence-based, truth-seeking, public interest investigative journalism, using a methodology which is rigorous and forensic.

In terms of academic research, my journalism has been empirical work, based on wide-ranging investigative research and extensive interviews. On reflection, it demonstrates evidence for and contributes to moral panic theory. Interestingly, I have discovered, the events I originally investigated very clearly illustrate a theory of 'explosive amplification' – when popular stories and official recognition – of an apparently new phenomenon coincide (Henningsen, 1980; Ellis, 2000, Hill, 2005,

2012) I discovered the concept of 'claims-makers' with missionary zeal, combined with other social factors – such as concern about child abuse – and crucially, an increasingly globalised mass media suddenly disseminating the story, could create a moral panic, for an apparent scare, for which there was little or no evidence. (deYoung, 2004; Richardson, 1991).

My continuing investigation into how the claims started, where, when, by whom, and why, and, over the years, how they spread, is empirical research. My article 'The Making of a Satanic Myth' (Waterhouse, 1990a) was an original contribution to knowledge at the time and has been cited internationally since.

This dissertation itself adds significantly to academic theories and historical accounts of these events, which occurred mainly from the early 1980s to late 1990s. Through a wide reading of the literature across the academic disciplines, I have pieced together a forensic chronology which I think provides a unique overview of a particular era of striking and peculiar phenomena. The more I researched for the dissertation, the more I could see that the 'Satanic panic' and inter-related psychotherapy fashions of recovered memory therapy and diagnosis of MPD/DID followed a pattern, which can be traced from the historical witch trials to modern day obsessions with 'historic' allegations of child abuse. After my research, I have concluded, the term 'moral panic' – as a concept – is highly appropriate for all these episodes.

My journalistic investigations into these inter-related phenomena have shared methodological and theoretical foundations based on established theories and practices of investigative journalism. The design and conduct of a long-term journalistic investigation does not have classic academic foundations like a social science survey or a psychological study into human beliefs or behaviour. Practical journalism is not a classic academic discipline. But it does have theoretical underpinnings. And, as explain in the dissertation, my own investigative journalistic methods follow a rigorous tradition of old-fashioned, tried and tested principles, aimed essentially at 'finding things out', (Peter Wilby, personal communication, confirmed by email November 2012), seeking the evidence, coming as I do from the school of truth-seeker (Pilger, 2004; Tofani, 1998; Evans, 1983) and detective (Bernstein and Woodward, 1974; Stotter, 2012), rather than campaigning 'muckraker' (Aucoin, 2007) or ventriloquist's dummy (Feldstein, 2007). However, as I reflect on how my journalism developed over the course of the investigations, in my occasional 'Satanic Panic' series for *Private Eye* since 2006 – the title comes from a 1993 book by Jeffrey S. Victor, *Satanic Panic: The Creation of a Contemporary Legend* – I can see that pure objectivity has sometimes given way to polemic, as particular stories have ignited my sense of moral outrage (Waterhouse, 2006a, 2006b, 2011, 2013a).

To summarise, the dissertation tells the story of the origins and spread of the Satanic panic and the crossover with the false/recovered memory movement; it chronicles my most significant publications and broadcast work on the topic since my first story in March 1990; and it analyses, explains and discusses *the process* of how I conducted the ongoing investigations. It analyses the data evidence and outcomes 24 years on – evaluating the evidence for the existence of Satanic ritual abuse and the current state of knowledge and professional beliefs about false and recovered memories and multiple personality disorder/ dissociative identity disorder (MPD/DID).

The dissertation explores how my published investigations relate to the academic literature in four key areas: the theory and practice of investigative journalism; the psychology of false and recovered memories; anomalistic psychology, the study of weird beliefs such as why people believe they have been abducted by aliens; and the sociology of moral panics.

Finally, it critically examines the impact of my published works in this field. I was one of the first journalists to conclude that, on the basis of the lack of corroborating evidence, after dozens of police investigations, in any case in the world that I was then aware of, that Satanic ritual abuse was a myth. Before my 'Making of a Satanic Myth' investigation in August 1990 (Waterhouse, 1990a), I was aware that a fellow investigative journalist, Debbie Nathan, had conducted a ground-breaking investigation into allegations in several cases in the US in the 1980s and had concluded there was no evidence to substantiate claims of a Satanic cult conspiracy. Nathan's article 'The Ritual Sex Abuse Hoax', published in the *Village Voice* in January 1990, had a strong influence on my thinking.

While I concluded there was no physical, corroborating evidence that Satanic ritual abuse existed, through my research and investigations, I was among the first researchers including journalists, police officers and academics able to show evidence for the origins and spread of the myth, identifying key events and people, both actual and metaphorical evangelical 'missionaries' (Best, 1990, 2001; Richardson, 1997, 2003) and 'claims-makers' (Best, 1990; Jenkins, 1992; Hill,1995a, 1995b, 1998; Cohen, 2002; Critcher, 2003).

Those spreading the scare comprised several distinct groups that formed loose alliances and reinforced each other's beliefs. Originally the main proponents were evangelical Christians, but they were soon joined by both secular and religious professionals including childcare workers and adult psychotherapists, 'anti-cult cops' and feminist activists. Word spread through so-called 'survivor' books and literature at seminars and conferences (Waterhouse, 1990a).

Claims of the existence of Satanic or ritual child abuse in the UK on a nationwide scale were first made widely public at a press conference of the National Society for the Prevention of Cruelty to Children to launch its annual report in March 1990. In the immediate aftermath the reaction of many childcare professionals and most in the media was credulous and uncritical. My own reports that week in my newspaper, the *Independent on Sunday*, concluded that 'evidence' of ritual abuse had been presented in at least five criminal cases and 14 wardship hearings involving 41 children in which children had been taken into care because of allegations of sexual abuse within the family.

But having been tasked by one of my editors to investigate this further, in August 1990, after a five-month investigation, I concluded in 'The Making of a Satanic Myth', published in the *Independent on Sunday* on 12 August, that Satanic ritual abuse did not exist as it had been described. I wrote that after dozens of investigations across the US, Canada and, in one case, in the

Netherlands, during the 1980s, and latterly in the UK, no physical, forensic, corroborating evidence had been found to substantiate the claims. (Lanning, 1989a; Hicks, 1989a, 1989b, 1990a 1990b, 1991, Mulhern, 1990). While always at pains to stress there was no doubting the sexual abuse of children was a widespread problem, and that Satanists do exist – some worship the Devil, and some practise black magic rituals – there was no evidence of an international conspiracy involving Satanists who sexually abused or sacrificed children as part of their beliefs.

In the course of that summer, a real-life Satanic panic broke out in Rochdale, Greater Manchester, when 20 children were taken into care in dawn raids by police and social workers amid allegations of Satanism and devil-worshipping after a six-year-old boy apparently spoke of a baby being born and killed, of ghosts and graves and sheep being stabbed and eaten. A judge ordered a ban on publicity and details of the case were not made public until September. Soon afterwards, the police announced that they had found no evidence of Satanism or any grounds for prosecution.

Soon after the Rochdale story broke, in a very rare occurrence involving rival newspapers, my 'Making of a Satanic Myth' investigation was republished almost in full on the leader page of the *Daily Mail*, on 15 September 1990, under the headline 'Death of a Satanic Myth', acknowledging the copyright of the *Independent on Sunday*.

Between August and October 1990 I wrote nine more in-depth articles investigating Satanic abuse stories which broke first in Rochdale and the Orkneys and in a TV documentary claiming to have evidence of Satanic abuse in a proven case of multi-generational incest in Nottingham (Waterhouse, 1990a, 1990b, 1990c, 1990d, 1990e, 1990f, 1990g, 1990h, 1990i, 1990j). On 21 October 1990 the *Mail on Sunday* produced a four-page Analysis feature 'The Attack on Innocence' (Walker et al., 1990) concluding that the notion of a highly organised network of Satanists sexually abusing children and sacrificing animals and babies was 'dangerous nonsense'. I was referenced in the introduction to this Analysis: 'We have been virtually alone in the national press in saying so – with the praiseworthy exception of Rosie Waterhouse in our rival newspaper, the *Independent on Sunday*.'

It was four more years before an official inquiry reached the same conclusion as I had, after Jean La Fontaine, emeritus professor of anthropology at the London School of Economics, investigated 84 cases alleged to have occurred in the UK between 1987 and 1992, involving police investigations and, in the most notorious cases of Rochdale and the Orkneys, children being seized in dawn raids by police officers and social workers, forcibly removed from their homes and taken into social services care. In her research findings, published in 1994, La Fontaine concluded there was no corroborating evidence that Satanic ritual abuse existed (Waterhouse, 1994a).

Over many years my work been cited by many academic researchers and journalists. (deYoung, 2004; Jenkins, 1992, ; Victor, 1991, 1992, 1994, 1996; Clapton, 1993; La Fontaine, 1998; Hill, 1998). This is the subject of the final section of this dissertation. I append a list of citations and publications which also include my contributions at conferences, and my chapter in the book *Investigative Journalism: Dead or Alive* (Mair and Keeble, 2011).

Contribution to knowledge

I have been a journalist since 1977, specialising in investigations – a member of the *Sunday Times* Insight team (twice), investigations editor of the *Independent on Sunday*, a BBC *Newsnight* reporter specialising in investigations and latterly (since becoming a senior lecturer in journalism at City University London, and director of the MA in Investigative Journalism) a freelance journalist specialising in investigative journalism, in particular on false allegations of sexual abuse.

I am internationally recognised as one of the first journalists and, indeed, any kind of researchers in the world to state unequivocally, in my first in-depth, longer-term investigation that, on the basis of available evidence, there was no corroborating, physical, forensic evidence to substantiate allegations of Satanic ritual abuse and to conclude, somewhat audaciously, after a mere five-month investigation, that it was a 'myth'. (Nathan, 1990, had described it as a hoax.)

In the course of researching this dissertation I have discovered that other journalists, especially in the US where the panic originated, were sceptical and conducted serious investigations questioning the evidence. Particularly impressive are Tom Charlier and Shirley Downing of the Memphis, Tennessee, *Commercial Appeal*, who in 1988 published a study of 36 cases of alleged ritual sexual abuse of children and concluded: 'Many of the stories labelled 'Satanic' or 'ritual'' have the hallmarks of urban legends.' (Victor, 1996, p.17).

Although I was not the first journalist to investigate the origins of the Satanic panic in the US, I was the first to reveal key details of how it spread to and within the UK. My feature 'The Making of a Satanic Myth' was published within five months of the sensational NSPCC claims, and, I believe, helped nip in the bud a potential full-scale 'moral panic'.

For this investigation I set out to conduct – in the limited time available for a newspaper story – what I wanted to be a definitive trawl of the evidence, from all available sources I could find, by tracing back from the beginning, the origins and sources of the NSPCC claims.

My research included evidence and findings from numerous police investigations in the US, Canada, the Netherlands and the UK. 'The Making of a Satanic Myth' has been much cited (deYoung, 2004; Jenkins, 1992, ; Victor, 1991, 1996; Clapton, 1993. La Fontaine, 1998 and Hill, 1998, cited its conclusion: 'Investigations have produced no evidence. No bodies, no bones, no bloodstains. Nothing.'

Alongside my investigations into the Satanic ritual abuse myth I became one of a very few UK journalists who came to specialise in a most unpopular area of journalism – investigating potentially false allegations of childhood sexual abuse. This took me into the world of the controversy over false versus recovered memories – a topic still hot in the worlds of psychiatry, psychology and psychotherapy. In the early 1990s I was the first national newspaper journalist to highlight a worrying new trend in the UK – of members of families, mostly ageing fathers, being accused by adult offspring of having sexually abused them as children, most often after having 'recovered' the suppressed memories during psychotherapy for mental health problems (Waterhouse, 1993a, 1993b, 1994e, 2011, 2013b; Waterhouse and Strickland, 1994). Some of these cases involved allegations of Satanic abuse. In the US, claims have been made that memories have been recovered of alien abduction. I would put both these phenomena in the same category of 'weird beliefs' in the unbelievable.

In the late 1990s I entered another highly controversial arena – 'historic' allegations of sexual abuse of children and young people in residential care homes in the 1970s and 1980s which led to a series of police investigations around the UK in the late 1990s. In a BBC *Newsnight* investigation in January 1997 I questioned whether some allegations of sexual abuse might be false, encouraged by police trawls for victims, including advertising in prison magazines, and child abuse lawyers advertising in local papers saying: 'Were you in these homes during these years? Were you abused?' and making clear the prospect of compensation (Waterhouse, 1997a).

In early 2013, following the publication of a joint report by the Metropolitan Police and the NSPCC, *Giving Victims a Voice*, on the extensive allegations of sexual abuse by the late Jimmy Savile over several decades I ventured into this highly controversial arena. I wrote in *Private Eye* that Valerie Sinason, a

Harley Street psychotherapist about whom I have written several articles in *Private Eye*, including Justice for Carol, claimed in a front page story in the *Sunday Express*, that Savile was 'Part of a Satanic Ring'. She based her claims on the cases of two patients who, she said, had recovered the memories 20 years later while in therapy with her (Waterhouse, 2013a).

Purpose of this PhD

What is the purpose of this PhD by Prior Publication? I think the purpose is two-fold. Primarily this PhD by Prior Publication is about investigative journalism. It is about my 24 years' worth of published journalism (my body of work), my investigation into Satanic ritual abuse and the controversy over false and recovered memories.

In the section on theoretical interpretations, under the sub-heading, how my published journalism on this topic relates to the theory and practice of investigative journalism, I address several questions: What is investigative journalism? What is my theory/model of investigative journalism? How does my theory and this on-going investigation relate to other forms of journalism and theories of investigative journalism? What is my contribution to knowledge about the 'Satanic panic' and the controversy over false versus recovered memories?

On my investigative journey for this dissertation I have had to research some of the vast literature on the psychology of recovered versus false memories, understand the different perspectives of the experimental and the clinical psychologists, the theories and practices of psychiatrists and psychotherapists and the dangerous and damaging teachings of and treatment by untrained and unqualified cranks and quacks. I particularly enjoyed discovering the literature in the field of anomalistic psychology – the study of weird beliefs, such as how and why people can come to believe they have been abducted by aliens. Some academics put a belief in Satanic ritual abuse in the same category (Holden and French, 2002; French, ;2009, 2013; Spanos et al., 1994; Showalter, 1997; McNally, 2003).

So for me, there is another purpose to this PhD by Prior Publication.

For more than 20 years as a journalist my job has been to report and investigate *what* and *how* things happened in the areas I came to specialise in – and decided to make the subjects of my body of work – the Satanic ritual abuse myth and the recovered versus false memory controversy. Therefore an important part of the purpose of my PhD by Prior Publication, for me, is to research and try to understand, possible explanations for *why* these events happened – *why* people behaved and believed as they did. And some still do.

PART 2

A summary of the origins and spread of the Satanic panic and some chief 'claims-makers'

Satanic ritual abuse: definitions.

I have defined Satanic ritual abuse as a belief in extreme sexual and physical abuse of children by organised networks and secret cults of devil worshipping Satanists, as part of their belief system, in bizarre black magic rituals which include the drinking of blood, eating of faeces, animal and human sacrifice and the impregnation of victims for the purpose of the breeding of babies for sacrifice (Waterhouse, 1990 to 2013).

A recognised official definition is:

Rites that allegedly include the torture and sexual abuse of children and adults, forced abortion and human sacrifice, cannibalism and bestiality may be labelled Satanic or Satanist.

Their defining characteristic is that the sexual and physical abuse of children is part of rites to a magical or religious objective. (La Fontaine, 1994).

La Fontaine investigated 84 alleged cases of Satanic abuse said to have occurred between 1987 and 1993, the most prominent of them in Nottingham, Rochdale and the Orkneys. She concluded there was no corroborating evidence of Satanic ritual abuse and identified three cases where rituals were used to frighten children and adults into submission and silence. She wrote:

Three substantiated cases of ritual, not Satanic, abuse were found. These are cases where self-proclaimed mystical/magical powers were used to entrap children and impress them (and also adults) with a reason for the sexual abuse, keeping the victim compliant and ensuring their silence. In these cases the ritual was secondary to the sexual abuse which clearly formed the primary objective of their perpetrators. (La Fontaine, 1994).

False memories and multiple personalities

Five books changed the worlds of psychiatry, psychology and psychotherapy and affected the lives of hundreds of thousands of people in different countries as belief in recovered, formerly repressed, memories of childhood sexual abuse, multiple personalities and, in extreme cases, Satanic abuse and alien abduction, spread around the world.

The books are: *The Three Faces of Eve* by Corbett H. Thigpen and Hervey M. Cleckley (1957), which was made into a film that became a box-office hit; *Sybil* by Flora Rheta Schreiber (1973), made into a TV film in 1976 and since convincingly exposed as a fraud (Nathan, 2011); the third edition of the American Psychiatric Association's *Diagnostic and Statistical Manual of Mental Disorders,* otherwise known as *DSM-III* (1980); *Michelle Remembers* by Michelle Smith and Lawrence Pazder (1980); and *The Courage to Heal: A Guide for Survivors of Child Sexual Abuse* by Ellen Bass and Laura Davis (1988).

'Eve' (real name Chris Costner Sizemore) made mainstream the concept of a patient with three personalities (no sexual abuse); 'Sybil' (Shirley Ardell Mason) had 16 personalities which emerged because of extreme childhood sexual and physical abuse; *DSM-III* introduced the diagnosis of multiple personality disorder; Michelle had recovered memories of childhood abuse by a Satanic cult; and *The Courage to Heal*, a self-help manual, made recovered memories mainstream.

Not all patients who 'recovered' memories of childhood sexual abuse were diagnosed as having multiple personalities. But, with one notable exception, 'Eve', all publicised diagnoses of MPD emerged in therapy along with recovered memories of childhood abuse. Sometimes all three elements were present – recovered memories of childhood abuse, involving Satanic cults and (sometimes) abductions by aliens in spaceships, and the emergence of multiple personalities.

Before 1944 there were just 76 cases of MPD reported (Taylor and Martin, 1944). Before 1970 there were a total of 79 well documented cases in the world literature (Lilienfeld and Lynn, 2003). Prior to 1980 there were around 200 (Bliss, 1980). By 1986 cases had risen to 6,000 (Coons, 1986). By the mid-1990s estimates put the number of MPD/DID cases at 40,000 in north America (Ross, 1997).

Sybil was not the only reason for the explosion of cases of recovered memories of childhood sexual abuse. The publication in 1980 by the American Psychiatric Association of the third edition of the *Diagnostic and Statistical Manual of Mental Disorders*, known as *DSM-III*, was also pivotal. This is the standard classification of mental disorders used by mental health professionals in the US and also internationally. For the first time *DSM-III* included a psychiatric condition then called multiple personality disorder, later to be re-named dissociative identity disorder (*DSM-IV*, 1994), which a small number of mental health professionals claimed resulted from extreme childhood trauma, notably sexual abuse. The proponents argued the condition occurred as a defence mechanism to suppress memories of abuse; the patient could only be healed by therapy to recover the memories.

From the early 1980s, psychiatrists, psychologists and psychotherapists – many of whom used hypnosis – latched on to the now-fashionable theory that extreme childhood trauma led to multiple personality disorder (a condition *DSM-III* originally stated was 'apparently extremely rare') and the self-proclaimed 'survivor' and 'recovered memory' movement mushroomed.

As cases of MPD spread like an epidemic after 1980, the authors of *The Three Faces of Eve*, Corbett Thigpen and Hervey Cleckley, tried to stop the contagion. In 1984 they published an article in the *International Journal of Clinical and Experimental Hypnosis*, 'On the Incidence of Multiple Personality Disorder: A Brief Communication':

Since reporting a case of multiple personality (Eve) over 25 years ago, we have seen many who were thought by others or themselves to have the disorder, but we have found only one case that fits the diagnosis... Over the past three decades we have together seen tens of thousands of psychiatric patients. Other than Eve, we have seen only one case (presented by a psychiatrist in Georgia) that appeared to be undeniably a genuine multiple personality. (Thigpen and Cleckley, 1984).

But by then it was too late. A whole new scientific – sceptics would say pseudoscientific – field had suddenly opened up. As the journalist Joan Acocella wrote in the *New Yorker* in 1998, the theory was the cause of MPD was acute childhood trauma, usually sexual abuse, and in order to cope the child imagined that the abuse was happening to someone else, another 'her', who then split off from the main personality, growing in isolation behind a wall of amnesia – a process called dissociation. As dissociation occurred again and again, the personalities multiplied, each developing its own name, nature and function.

Bolstered by the inclusion of MPD in *DSM-III* in 1980, a close-knit group of psychiatrists and therapists, including Cornelia Wilbur (the therapist of 'Sybil'), formed the International Society for the Study of Multiple Personality and Dissociation (ISSMP+D), and in 1984 began holding annual conferences co-sponsored by Rush-Presbyterian-St Luke's Medical Center, based at Rush University in Chicago, and chaired by Dr Bennett G. Braun, one of the foremost proponents of MPD. Rush-Presbyterian opened the first dissociative disorders unit, under Braun, other units followed around north America, and this new and expanding field launched its own journal, *Dissociation*, in 1988, peer-reviewing contributions, with Braun as its founding editor.

The most evangelical advocates of MPD contributed chapters to the 1986 book, *Treatment of Multiple Personality*, edited by Braun, the first book authored by clinicians published since the story of Sybil. (The first published references to widespread recovered memories of 'Satanic abuse' appeared in this book in a chapter by Braun.) Most of its contributors went on to become the most prolific publishers of research and academic papers in support of MPD and DID. They include Cornelia Wilbur, Richard Kluft, Roberta Sachs, Frank Putnam and David Spiegel, who led the recent campaign to retain DID in the fifth edition of the *Diagnostic and Statistical Manual of Mental Disorders*, published in May 2013.

I focused on the origins and spread of the diagnoses of MPD and DID in a *New Scientist* feature (Waterhouse, 2013) based on a talk I gave to the Anomalistic Psychology Research Unit at Goldsmith's, University of London (run by Professor Christopher French, who is also external supervisor of my PhD by Prior Publication). I examine some of the research into the validity of MPD and DID in the section of this dissertation on how my journalism relates to the academic literature on false versus recovered memories.

Satan arrives on the scene

Claims of Satanic ritual abuse can be traced to the publication in 1980 of *Michelle Remembers* by Michelle Smith and Lawrence Pazder.

This purported to be Smith's true 'survivor' story – of how, after a miscarriage and 200 hours of therapy, she recovered previously forgotten memories of being tormented during her childhood by nightmarish, perverted sexual abuse by a Satanic cult which imprisoned her for several months during 1955, when she was five years old (Waterhouse, 1990a). She completely forgot the experiences for more than 20 years until she entered therapy with Pazder, whom she later married and with whom she co-wrote the book (Smith and Pazder, 1980). The book became an international best-seller but has subsequently been thoroughly discredited (Nathan and Snedeker 1995, pp.45-46).

The book is an almost pornographic 'misery memoir' – little Michelle, aged five, being tortured, raped, sodomised with candles, being forced to defecate on a Bible and a crucifix, witnessing babies and adults butchered and sacrificed, spending hours naked in a snake-filled cage, and having a devil's tail and horns surgically attached to her. These 'grotesque abuses' are said to have gone on for almost a year, until Michelle's indomitable Christian faith, with the actual physical intervention of Jesus and the Virgin Mary, defeated the Satanists and the Devil himself (Nathan and Snedeker, 1995; Hill, 1998). Smith and Pazder became the earliest 'claims-makers' or 'missionaries' who were to spread the Satanic panic.

Smith and Pazder went to the Vatican to alert the church about the dangers to children from Satanic cults worldwide, and to warn the world they wrote *Michelle Remembers*. Exactly how and where and with whom the full Satanic ritual abuse scenario originated remains a mystery. Nathan and Snedeker (1995) claim Pazder was the first person to coin the phrase 'ritual abuse' at the 134th annual meeting of the American Psychiatric Association in New Orleans in May 1981. A programme for the 1981 APA annual meeting lists an evening event on May 14 entitled 'Michelle Remembers: New Frontiers in Psychiatry', with Pazder billed as moderator and Smith as a participant (Pazder, 1981). Some researchers have noted that Pazder was a devoutly Christian psychiatrist (Guilliatt,1996); others have speculated that Pazder's interest in cults stemmed from his time working as a medical practitioner in west Africa in the early 1960s 'at a time of great public concern over secret cannibalistic cults'. (Barnett and Hill, 1993).

After publication of *Michelle Remembers* allegations of Satanic ritual abuse of children in nurseries and daycare centres began to emerge in the US, with the first case beginning in 1983 at the McMartin pre-school in Manhattan Beach, Los Angeles, California, after a mother, who turned out to be a mentally ill alcoholic, reported to police that her son had been sexually assaulted by a male member of staff in a particularly sadistic manner. According to the journalist Debbie Nathan, in her seminal investigation published in *Village Voice* in January 1990, the police wrote to 200 parents asking them to question their children to find out whether they had been molested. Leading interviews then followed with social workers suggesting ritual scenarios; denial was taken as confirmation (Nathan, 1990). Pazder met parents and therapists in 1984 as an expert on Satanic ritual abuse. (Nathan and Snedeker, 1995, p.89). The stage was set for the longest and most expensive trial in US criminal history at a cost of $15 million (*New York Times*, 24 January 1990) and a nationwide panic about ritual abuse in daycare centres. Initially seven people were arrested – 62-year-old Peggy McMartin Buckey, her son Raymond and five female childcare workers accused of 321 counts of sexually assaulting children – more than 150 were allegedly abused (Guilliat, 1996). By the time the case went to trial in 1987, charges had been dropped against the five childcare workers, and after the first, 28-month, trial Peggy McMartin Buckey was acquitted. The jury reached not guilty and hung verdicts on Raymond Buckey. At his second trial in 1990 there was a hung verdict and the charges were finally dismissed, allowing Buckey to be released after languishing five years in prison. (Nathan and Snedeker, 1995, p.92).

The McMartin allegations attracted nationwide attention in the media and in professional childcare, police and adult therapy circles. Nathan (1990) estimated that during investigations into subsequent allegations of Satanic ritual abuse in daycare centres in the US between 1984 and 1989 about 100 people were charged with ritual sex abuse. Of those, she wrote, around 50 were tried and about half convicted 'with no evidence except testimony from children, parents, 'experts' expounding on how the children acted traumatised' and dubious medical evidence.

In their riveting account of the ritual abuse daycare centre panic in north America in the 1980s and 1990s, *Satan's Silence: Ritual Abuse and the Making of a Modern American Witch Hunt* (1995), Nathan and Michael Snedeker, a defence lawyer, provide a succinct and comprehensive explanation for the phenomenon:

Belief in ritual-sex abuse conspiracies was the stuff of moral panic. . . This is the way belief in ritual abuse spread: via an impassioned, nationwide crusade conducted by social workers, therapists, physicians, victimology researchers, police, criminal prosecutors, fundamentalist Christians, ambitious politicians, anti-pornography campaigners, feminists and the media. It was a powerful effort that did not come together overnight. But as it took shape, a veritable industry developed around the effort to demonstrate the existence of ritual abuse. In the absence of conventional evidence, the proof became words obtained via suggestion and coercion and the most ambiguous of behaviours, from both youngsters and the accused. Verbal 'disclosures' about events that never happened were obtained from children using interview techniques that cognitive psychologists have subsequently discredited as dangerously coercive and suggestive. Additionally, prosecutors introduced new forms of therapeutically induced 'evidence' – such as preschool-age children's play with toys and dolls that have genitals, their vague scribbles and drawings, and parents' retrospective accounts of their children's nightmares and masturbation – to show that the youngsters had been traumatised by abuse. (Nathan and Snedeker, 1995, pp.4-5).

One of the earliest researchers into the 'Satanic panic' – a term he coined in his 1993 book of that title – was Jeffrey S. Victor, who published a paper in January 1990, 'Satanic Cult Rumors as Contemporary Legend'. Victor describes his research, begun in 1988, into a 'rumor-panic' in one small city, Jamestown, New York. Rumours had been circulating widely in the community about a supposedly dangerous Satanic cult in the vicinity. Research, initially from stories in newspapers, revealed the rumour-panic was 'national in scope' and included the daycare ritual abuse cases which, he writes, 'swept across the country'.

Under the heading 'The Transmission of the Satanic Cult Legend', Victor lists the common sources for the spread and promotion of the 'Satanic cult legend'. These included:

Police seminars and public conferences about Satanic cult crime; conferences on child sexual abuse having presentations about ritual child abuse; conferences of anti-cult organisations; church and revival meetings; the media including newspaper and popular magazines, television talk shows, true crime books, religious books, Christian radio programs and magazines; so-called experts including police officers and clergy, adult Satanic cult survivors, often claiming to be suffering from multiple personality disorder (MPD) as a direct consequence of suffering ritual abuse and the psychotherapists who believe their stories and publish reports about ritual abuse; child advocates and anti-cult volunteers who lecture about Satanic cult ritual child abuse. (Victor, 1990a, pp.76-78).

In another article in 1990, 'The Spread of Satanic Cult Rumors', Victor wrote: 'I have been trained as a sociological researcher, which means that I investigate the causes of group behaviour. A rumor-panic is much like the stampede of a herd of buffalo: It is a product of group force rather than of the personal motives of individuals.' (Victor, 1990b, p.287).

In a concise and entertaining overview, 'Satan's Excellent Adventure in the Antipodes', published in 1998, a British-born sociologist, Michael Hill, traces the origins and spread of the 'Satanism scare' from North America to Australia and New Zealand (and also the UK) by a small but key group of 'claims-makers'. 'To date there is no physical corroboration of the atrocities allegedly perpetrated by these Satanists,' he wrote (Hill, 1998). Later, in the context of the New Zealand Christchurch Civic Crèche case he wrote unequivocally, on the basis of two official US and UK government reports published in 1994, and his own researches: 'It is therefore deeply ironic that against the stark reality of child abuse there was introduced to New Zealand from 1990 onwards the scenario of a novel but *entirely fictional* [my italics] form of abuse known as Satanic ritual abuse.' (Hill, 2005).

One of the earliest researchers in this field, Hill started out specialising in the sociology of religion and later deviance, and is today an emeritus professor in the School of Social and Cultural Studies, Victoria University, Wellington, New Zealand. In the early 1990s while on a sabbatical, he worked in London at Inform, a unit which studied alternative religions and cults, based at the London School of Economics, and became familiar with the research then being undertaken by Professor Jean la Fontaine for her government inquiry into the existence of Satanic ritual abuse (La Fontaine, 1994, 1998). He is highly knowledgeable about the Satanic panics in the US, UK, Australia and New Zealand (Hill, 1992, 1994, 1995a, 1995b, 1998, 2005, Barnett and Hill, 1993). Along with most other specialist researchers on this topic, he classes the Satanic ritual abuse myth as a moral panic, spread by 'claims-makers', a theory I return to below.

The Satanic abuse daycare cases involving children and the epidemic of multiple personality disorder diagnosed in adults recovering 'memories' in therapy – including alleged memories of Satanic ritual abuse – reinforced each other (Mulhern, in Waterhouse, 1990a, Mulhern 1991, 1994). Hill cites a study of early modern witch hunts in which Gustav Henningsen uses the term 'explosive amplification' to describe the moment when popular accounts and beliefs (*Michelle Remembers*) and officialdom (*DSM-III*) fuse together and trigger a witch hunt – and argues that this is what happened with the Satanic ritual abuse scare, which spread firstly through fundamentalist Christian channels (Waterhouse, 1990a) and was then validated by a group of secular professionals, especially those involved in adult psychotherapy (Mulhern, 1991; Hill, 1998), social workers, childcare professionals and 'cult cops' (Waterhouse, 1990b; Lanning, 1991; Hicks, 1991), and by the feminist movement (Guillatt, 1996).

In his seminal articles on the 'Satanism scare', and its international 'diffusion' from America, with anti-Satanism as his central theme and conduit, the sociologist James T. Richardson (1991, 1997, 2009) lists key factors which he argues 'contributed to the rise of the moral panic concerning Satanism in America' and elsewhere including: the existence of Satanist churches, proving Satanists actually existed; the rise of Christian fundamentalism which posits a real Satan, active in the world; development of a 'child saver' movement; emergence of the adult 'occult survivor' of alleged Satanic activities and the related 'repressed memory' phenomena; mass media promotion of Satanism, using modern technologies such as satellite and cable television; helping professionals such as social work, law enforcement, and psychotherapy, accepting Satanism as real, and promoting such ideas through professional activities such as continuing education training; the rise of feminism as a social movement; and the spread of Satanism around the Western world, promoted in large part by American anti-Satanist 'missionaries' and globalised mass media.

International spread

A small but vocal number of 'claims-makers' or 'missionaries' embarked on the international conference circuit, wrote books and papers for academic journals to spread the word about this apparently new bizarre and previously hidden form of sadistic child abuse by an international network of Satanic cults. The panic spread from Canada and North America and led to a series of police investigations, starting in Oude Pekela in the Netherlands in 1987 (Jonker, 1989) and continuing with cases in Congleton, Cheshire in the UK in 1987 (La Fontaine, 1994); Sydney, Australia, in 1988, then around the country; Christchurch, New Zealand, in 1991 (Hill, 1998); Bjugn in Norway in 1992; Munster, Germany, in 1993; and Stockholm, Sweden in 1993 (Holgerson, 1995). As Hill wrote in his wry account of 'Satan's Excellent Adventure in the Antipodes', what he calls the 'Satanism scare'

began in north America in the early 1980s, arrived in Australia during the late 1980s and in New Zealand from 1990 onwards. Its importation was associated with conference presentations and published material by a small but key group of claims-makers, several of whom had been associated with the earlier McMartin preschool investigation (in Manhattan Beach, California in 1983. (Hill, 1998)

Hill identifies four main Satanic abuse claims-makers from the McMartin case who exported the notion around the world:

- Kee MacFarlane, a social worker and interviewer;
- Roland Summit, a psychiatrist who coined the 'pseudoscientific' term 'The Child Sexual Abuse Accommodation Syndrome' in a paper written in 1978 and widely distributed prior to its eventual publication in 1983, in which he argued that children never lied about abuse, and therefore must be believed, but that children who had been victims of incest would often retract to maintain family 'equilibrium', and so a denial of abuse should not be believed, (Summit, 1983);
- David Finkelhor, a New Hampshire sociologist, who gathered evidence of daycare cases in the US between 1983 and 1985, and found some 'three dozen ritual abuse scandals', which he then wrote about in a co-authored book *Nursery Crimes* (Finkelhor, Williams and Burns, 1988) which became 'a Bible for ritual abuse believers' (Nathan and Snedeker, 1995, p.132);
- Dr. Astrid Heger, who popularised diagnostic techniques for identifying abuse which were later discredited (Nathan and Snedeker, 1995, pp.197-198).

MacFarlane, Summit, Finkelhor and Heger all gave presentations on their work on the McMartin case at the Sixth International Conference on Child Abuse and Neglect in Sydney in August 1986, the largest in Australia's history (Guilliat, 1996). Hill says that there were 'fascinating links and parallels' between the McMartin case and the first case involving allegations of Satanic abuse, in Sydney in 1988'.

Three other Americans became prolific claims-makers around the world. Pamala Klein, a rape crisis worker from Chicago who settled in the UK in 1985, set up a consultancy with Norma Howes, an independent social worker with whom she organised two of the earliest conferences in the UK to raise claims of Satanic ritual abuse, in Reading and Dundee in 1989. Klein became involved in introducing the notion of Satanic abuse in cases, notably in Nottingham, Epping Forest and Kent (Waterhouse 1990d, 1990e, 1991a, 1991b, 1991c). Pamela Hudson, a social worker, and Catherine Gould, a clinical psychologist, both from California, produced lists of so-called Satanic indicators, lists of signs and symptoms to look for, which became widely disseminated at conferences around the world. REFS Hudson and Gould

According to Hill (1995a), writing about the Christchurch civic crèche case,

Pamala Klein was only the first in a succession of true believers in the Satanic ritual abuse scenario to be brought to

New Zealand. Others included Pamela Hudson – a Californian social worker who wrote books and articles on Satanic ritual abuse which have provided a 'script' for subsequent investigators and believers. She was invited to Christchurch by the Campbell Centre in late 1993. Another Californian, Roland Summit (a believer in the existence of tunnels under a California crèche which suffered a Satanic panic – despite police failure to locate them), was invited to New Zealand by Doctors for Sexual Abuse Care.

The Satanic cult scenario was imported to the UK and elsewhere through the same channels – conferences, 'survivor' books and claims-makers. Among the earliest claims-makers in the UK were Dianne Core, founder of a children's charity, Childwatch, and a freelance journalist, Fred Harrison, who first started spreading stories of ritual abuse and sacrifice in newspapers in the UK in the late 1980s. Core also went on the international circuit. In an interview with the American magazine *New Federalist* in November 1988 she claimed 4,000 children a year were being sacrificed in Satanic rituals in the UK alone (Burdman, 1998). She repeated this claim at a conference in Rome in January 1989 (Core 1989).

Norway was introduced to the notion of Satanic ritual abuse in March 1990 (Dyrendal, 2005) following the widespread publicity surrounding claims made by the UK NSPCC (see below) which were reported by the Norwegian newspaper *Dagenand Dagbladet* (Norway's third largest newspaper). Dyrendal reveals *Dagbladet* then ran a longer piece on 11 August 1990 by the freelance journalist Fred Harrison on the English Satanic ritual abuse claims featuring an interview with a British psychiatrist, Dr Victor Harris, which included claims of 'Satanic mind control cults among the powerful'.

Harris was an important early 'claims-maker' in the UK. He was then based at a hospital in the town of Rochdale where one of the most notorious cases of false allegations of Satanic ritual abuse began in June 1990 (though it was made public only in September 1990). On 19 August, the week following my article in the *Independent on Sunday*, 'The Making of a Satanic Myth' (Waterhouse, 1990a), Harris had a letter to the editor published in my newspaper in which he said he was treating a patient, Sara, who was reporting to him 'ritual abuse suffered from the age of four to the present day' and that she had 'bravely' publicised her plight in the *News of the World* to warn off the cult. And yet in his letter he conceded my article on Satanic abuse 'rightly points out that all allegations of such abuse are unsupported by evidence'. (Harris, 1990).

According to Dyrendal, in his feature interview with Harris in *Dagbladet*, Harrison disclosed that he and Core 'were also following leads to Norway'. Dyrendal (2005) writes that in June 1991 Harrison and Core joined forces with a Norwegian police officer who, in an interview with *Dagbladet* , claimed to be investigating claims of a Satanic abuse 'survivor'. Soon more 'survivors' came forward.

In summer 1991, Core and Harrison's book, *Chasing Satan: An investigation into Satanic Crimes Against Children*, was published. Quite how or why Core and Harrison got involved with or introduced tales of Satanic ritual abuse to Norway I have not discovered. But Norway features in their book: chapter nine, 'The Nordic Trail: Sex and the Serpent'. Like *Michelle Remembers*, the content is bordering on pornography. 'She was a 13 year-old virgin when he first took her to bed. It was just the two of them. And a snake.' (Core and Harrison, 1991, p.97).

The story claims (pp.97-98) that the sexual abuse of this 'victim', who Core and Harrison called 'Kari', continued until she was 15, she became pregnant, the five-month-old baby was aborted, cut with a knife, the foetus drained of blood; Kari was taken to a basement , full of about 20 men, laid out on a stone and an orgy commenced. 'The spiritual consummation of her seduction was the ritual sex with men who believed she had been impregnated by the devil. To this day she cannot understand the significance of the snake.' The chapter goes on to describe how other Satanic abuse 'survivors' related their 'relationship with

Lucifer' to a chief inspector in the Oslo police force child abuse unit. Norway's only 'ritual abuse' case at a kindergarten in Bjugn followed in 1992. The influence of therapist Kee MacFarlane, involved in interviewing children in the McMartin case, was mentioned in news reports (Dyrendal, 2005).

In a hard-hitting paper, 'Professionals as Evaluators or Indoctrinators in Sex Abuse Cases', (1995), Astrid Holgerson, a Swedish witness psychologist who has studied the cases in Germany, Norway and Sweden, argues that many professionals in sexual abuse cases—psychologists, psychiatrists, social workers and police officers – typically used 'unethical, manipulative methods and even lies to get the child to tell'. She is particularly scathing about the interviewing methods advocated by Tilman Furniss, a German professor of child and adolescent psychiatry and prominent claims-maker, then (1995) based at Munster University. According to Holgerson, Furniss had previously worked in both Amsterdam and London, and she claimed that his interview methods to 'make children tell' had 'infected' professionals in other countries including those involved in the cases in Norway, Germany and Sweden. Holgerson blamed Furniss's 'proselytising' influence for spreading the scare. She wrote: 'The so-called hypothetical questioning has been introduced and promoted by a highly manipulative 'indoctrinator' in the field of child sexual abuse. His name is

Tilman Furniss and he is supposed to be a professional expert – which makes his work extremely dangerous.'

Another significant influence on the international spread was the publication in 1988 of *The Courage to Heal: A Guide for Survivors of Child Sexual Abuse*, written by Ellen Bass and Laura Davis, which became an international best seller. Popularised by the feminist movement, it was a promoted as a self-help book for 'survivors' of incest and childhood sexual abuse, including Satanic ritual abuse, and for people who developed multiple personalities to 'wall off' the memories.

PART 3

My investigations into the myth

This section tells the story of my investigations over more than two decades into the Satanic ritual abuse myth and the controversy over false versus recovered memories. It explains the design and methodology of this journalistic investigation, and some principles of journalistic investigations in general, as opposed to pure social sciences research. I focus on my first two investigations (Waterhouse et al., 1990; Waterhouse, 1990a), though I also refer to the most significant of my numerous other publications over the years, outlining the general principles of the methodology and conduct of research.

How it happened

The story of my investigation began on Monday 12 March 1990 with sensational claims by the NSPCC that child protection workers were encountering a new and horrific form of child sexual abuse by cults of devil-worshipping paedophiles in bizarre occult rituals that included the drinking of blood and urine, the smearing of children with excrement and the sacrifice of animals and humans, with babies being bred for the purpose.

In the days long before the internet and online news outlets, the 24-hour news agency, the Press Association, was the first media organisation to report the news, via its subscription wire service, soon after the event. 'Children as young as five are being forced to take part in bizarre sex and Satanic rituals, the National Society for the Prevention of Cruelty to Children warned today. Rites involved drugs, animal sacrifice and the drinking of urine and blood', the PA story said under the headline 'Children Forced into Evil Sex Rites'. 'The NSPCC has called for police and government action after examples of ritualistic abuse were reported by seven of its (66) investigating teams.'

The shocking claims were made by the charity's childcare director, Jim Harding, at a press conference to launch its annual report – always a high-profile event geared to maximise publicity and fundraising for the charity's work.

The following morning the daily newspapers duly reported as grim fact the authoritative words of a respected official of a revered children's charity. The headlines were startling. 'NSPCC says Child Abuse Rife' (*Times*); 'Children Abused in Bizarre Sex

Rituals', (*Independent*); 'NSPCC Uncovers 'Satanic' Abuse' (*Guardian*).

The claims about ritual abuse were not made in the annual report itself, but reported by Harding reading from a briefing note at the press conference. I later discovered in an interview with an NSPCC press officer that some of the claims were so shocking as to be barely credible and Harding did not hand out the briefing note. But as I found out from the NSPCC press officer, the reporter from the *Daily Mirror* saw details in the notes including claims that four of the seven teams reported that children had spoken of human sacrifice.

So the *Mirror* (then boasting the previous day's sales, incorporating the Scottish *Daily Record*, were 3,908,222) went much further than the rest and gave the story by far the most lurid treatment. Under the front-page banner headline 'KIDS FORCED INTO SATAN ORGIES', with a sub-heading 'Sex slaves' ordeal exposed by NSPCC' the paper wrote:

The shocking rites of Satanist cults are exposed by the NSPCC who questioned more than 20 victims. Youngsters told of CHILDREN being made to eat part of a 'human' heart. A BABY being seen in a microwave oven and another in a deep freeze. Up to 20 children at a time took part in orgies in which masks and costumes were worn, blood and urine were drunk and animals were tortured and killed. (Todd, 1990)

The *Mirror* quoted Harding as saying: 'We believe the children's accounts ... They are obviously talking about very painful experiences that it would have been impossible to make up.'

The reporter, Roger Todd, then quoted even more extraordinary claims from another source, who was not present at the press conference, Maureen Davies, director of the Reachout Trust, a counselling organisation which helped people escape from occult cults. She 'believes Satanists carry out ritual murders', he wrote, and went on:

The victims are often homeless youngsters. Foetuses are also sacrificed. Mrs Davies has details of a 19 year-old girl who was introduced to a Satanic group by her parents. She was made pregnant five times from the age of 14. When she was five and a half months pregnant the birth would be induced. The live baby was placed on an altar and sacrificed. After her last pregnancy she had to kill her own baby. (Todd, 1990)

The *Mirror* report then returned to the 'harrowing devil worship dossier' that was 'part of an NSPCC probe into organised child abuse throughout England, Wales and Northern Ireland', giving the clear impression of a potentially nationwide conspiracy. The NSPCC director, Christopher Brown, 'revealed that his organisation is joining forces with government officials and the police to combat the evil'. However, as the reporter had to concede: 'But so far the police have not been able to unearth PROOF.'

All the papers that day had reported that the police had, so far, found no evidence. And with hindsight, it's clear that journalists following this story thereafter should have employed rather more scepticism and started asking: 'What's the evidence?'

In fairness to my editors at the *Independent on Sunday* (newly launched in January 1990), they decided to investigate exactly what we could establish was the evidence for the existence of what became known as Satanic ritual abuse in the short time available before the following Sunday's paper.

Sunday newspaper reporters did not usually attend press conferences which would be reported in the daily papers so I was not present at the headline-hitting NSPCC 'presser' on Monday 12 March. (It was also my day off.)

But because the morning papers of Tuesday 13 March were so full of reports on the story, at the regular morning news conference that day at the *Independent on Sunday*, attended by senior editors and correspondents, the topic of Satanic ritual abuse was included when the tentative preliminary news list was drawn up.

Two staff reporters were put on the job. Then employed as a general news reporter, I was chosen because of my strong background in investigations, most recently as a member of the *Sunday Times* Insight Team. I was tasked to investigate the evidence for the existence of Satanic ritual abuse. Sharon Kingman, health correspondent, was to research the question: 'Can children be trusted to tell the truth?' As part of my background research I used the newspaper cuttings service then called Lexis Nexis (now Nexis UK), one of the first online databases of the archives of journalistic publications to trawl for any previous stories using the search terms 'ritual abuse' and 'Satanic abuse', both terms used by the NSPCC.

In the course of this search I found reference to a story by a freelance journalist, Jenny Cuffe, who had researched and presented an investigative feature broadcast on Radio Four *Woman's Hour* on 30 January 1990 on the topic 'Ritual child abuse' (Cuffe, 1990). I made contact with her, and agreed the *Independent on Sunday* would pay her a fee for background information. Her sources and contacts proved to be extremely helpful.

The programme included interviews with people who would later prove to be key proponents who played an active role in spreading sensational stories about Satanic abuse. So we three shared a by-line on a package of stories on page 5 – 'Rosie Waterhouse, Sharon Kingman and Jenny Cuffe on the evidence behind this week's NSPCC report' (Waterhouse, Kingman and Cuffe, 1990). I soon came to regret what we wrote.

The headline was typical of the rather cerebral and literary-minded *Independent on Sunday*: 'A Satanic Litany of Children's Suffering'. There was a rather more attention-grabbing sub-heading: 'Sexual perversion, animal sacrifice and the drinking of blood are among bizarre rituals adding a shocking new dimension to abuse of the young.' There was a panel of cases compiled by me of criminal convictions which included allegations of Satanic or ritual abuse, with the heading 'Evidence of evil'. And there was a photograph of a Church of England vicar, interviewed by me, with a caption saying: 'The Rev Kevin Logan says girls have been impregnated so that their foetuses could be sacrificed.'

In the course of that week's research I was at great pains to focus on evidence. These allegations involved violent and bloody crimes including sexual assaults and even murder. In the few days available for research I thought it was feasible that I could do a newspaper archives search on Lexis Nexis to see if there had been newspaper reports in the UK regional or national newspapers of any criminal prosecutions which involved allegations of ritualistic Satanic abuse. My search revealed five, duly reported under the headline 'Evidence of Evil'.

I then decided to find out whether allegations of Satanic abuse featured in any 'child abuse within the family' wardship cases. For this information I contacted the office of the Official Solicitor and struck what I thought was a goldmine. Jim Baker, the deputy Official Solicitor, told me that about a year earlier his staff began to notice references to bizarre and disturbing accusations of sexual abuse with ritualistic overtones and so he started a separate file of these cases. This showed that in the previous two years allegations of Satanism, black magic and witchcraft had featured in 14 wardship cases involving 41 children taken into care after allegations of sexual abuse.

This was convincing material. But as I later realised, verbal, anecdotal 'evidence' given in court is not the same as physical, forensic, corroborating evidence which would constitute proof. There followed in the article a paragraph of comment which has since proved to be entirely wrong. I cannot recall whether I wrote this or whether it was inserted by my news editor. It stated unequivocally: 'Because children are not always believed, and because the practices alleged are carried out in the utmost secrecy, hard evidence is often lacking; *but the existence of ritualistic abuse on a disturbing scale is beyond dispute.*' (My italics.)

Just five months later, after I was commissioned to conduct a longer-term investigation to try to discover the true nature of the evidence and scale of Satanic ritual abuse, my newspaper carried a full page feature under the headline 'The Making of a Satanic myth' with a sub-heading 'Adult 'survivors' tell horrific tales of ritual child abuse but the evidence is missing.'

An eye-catching pullquote from the article stated: 'Investigations have produced no evidence. No bodies, no bones ... no bloodstains. Nothing.' (Waterhouse, 1990a).

This investigation is now accepted as a seminal piece of journalism quoted by fellow journalists and academics who have researched the phenomenon of Satanic ritual abuse citations include deYoung, 2004; Jenkins, 1992, ; Victor, 1991, 1996; Clapton, 1993; La Fontaine, 1998; and Hill, 1998.

In order to understand how a newspaper – and indeed this reporter – could move from one end of the spectrum of belief to the other in the space of five months, in the following section I explain the design and methodology for those two investigations and the conduct of the research. I then explain how and why I continued to investigate stories in this field over the next almost 24 years.

Methodology and conduct of research

Methodology

I did not begin to study the academic literature on journalistic methodology until I started teaching in 2003.

I trained through the traditional route of practical journalism as an 'indentured' trainee on the *Chester Chronicle*, a weekly newspaper, following a five-month course at the Thomson Regional Newspapers training centre in Cardiff starting in January 1977. After the initial training course – covering the essentials of reporting news, public administration, media law and shorthand – I literally learned on the job, though over the years I did derive inspiration and some general principles on conducting an investigation from books such as *All the President's Men* (Bernstein and Woodward,1974) and *Good Times, Bad Times* (Evans, 1983). In the course of research for this dissertation I have of course studied in more detail some essential reading on classic investigative journalism methodology which I will address in the section on the theory and practice of investigative journalism.

The journalistic method of conducting research may be less formulaic than pure social science research but in some respects, in terms of planning and conducting your investigation, there are many similarities – just different terminology to describe it. Bell

(2010) helpfully argues that no approach prescribes nor automatically rejects any particular method of conducting an investigation – but there is a process. The basic questions any reporter sets out to answer in the course of researching anything from a simple news story to a complex investigation are: What (happened)? When? Where? Who? How? and, my favourite, Why?

In the course of my journalistic career I have seen how some journalists and editors begin with a theory and select facts to fit. In my mind this is bad practice. On an in-depth investigation such as 'The Making of a Satanic Myth' I started out with the sole purpose of finding out 'What's the evidence for the existence of Satanic ritual abuse?' The conduct of a long-term investigation involves the same process as that required for researching a piece of analysis or feature. This process could be said to follow the lines of an acronym, IRASS: Idea, Research, Assimilation, Structure and Style. I was introduced to this acronym when I started teaching journalism at City University London in 2003 by the then-director of the newspaper journalism course, Linda Christmas. I have been unable to find any other references to IRASS. But it is a neat reminder for students – and working journalists – of the stages of producing a feature or investigation. I was not aware of it when I was a full-time working journalist. But it is the process I had learned to follow.

Once given the 'Idea' to investigate, the journalistic method begins with drawing up a list of tasks – sources to research and people to interview. This 'to do' list is added to as research progresses. The classic methodology of any longer feature or investigation is firstly to 'check the cuts' – that is review all previous published journalism on the topic in the UK and if relevant internationally (the journalistic equivalent of conducting a critical review of the academic literature). This review of previously published journalism will lead to further sources and experts to pursue and people to interview. After this initial background research the next stage would be interviewing all people and organisations with any knowledge of the allegations/cases, including those making the allegations, those accused and their supporting campaign groups, and those investigating the allegations including the police, psycho-medical professionals and lawyers; using sources who bring material to the journalist; and finding 'experts' ranging from academics to vicars and priests. The final stage of each investigation is to write the story, the process of which can be a challenge in itself – What material to use? What to discard? Should I remain 'objective' or select the facts that fit an argument?

Having read some of the literature on planning a social science research project I see strong similarities with planning a journalistic investigation.

In *Doing Your Research Project* (2010, fifth edition), Judith Bell outlines basic principles which are directly applicable to a journalistic investigation: 'Regardless of your topic or discipline, the problems facing you will be much the same. You will need to select a topic, identify the objectives of your study, plan and design a suitable methodology, devise research instruments, negotiate access to institutions, materials and people, collect, analyse and present information, and, finally, produce a well written report.'(p.1). This is precisely the same process as set out in the acronym IRASS – Idea, Research, Assimilation, Structure and Style.

In describing how to plan an investigation she refers to 'well-established and well-reported styles of research' from 'quantitative researchers' who collect data and facts 'and study the relationship of one set of facts to another' and researchers adopting a 'qualitative perspective', more concerned to understand individuals' perceptions of the world. In her analysis of 'Qualitative Methods in the Study of News', Gaye Tuchman (1991) argues that, in her experience of the study of news, the most valuable and significant research is qualitative, based on historical inquiry, interviews and participant observation.

In my experience a good journalistic investigation requires both the quantitative and qualitative approaches in order to see both the bigger picture and the human experience.

In Bell's chapter on 'Planning the Project', the steps are the same as for a journalistic investigation: select a topic; ask yourself what's the purpose of the study – in the case of the main longer term investigation discussed here (Waterhouse, 1990a) it is to find out what's the evidence for the existence of Satanic ritual abuse. Then you can possibly explore hypotheses, but certainly set out your objectives and researchable questions.

In the introduction to the chapter 'Selecting Methods of Data Collection', Bell advises: 'The initial question is not 'Which methodology?' but 'What do I need to know and why?' Only then do you ask 'What is the best way to collect information?' Stages in both types of research typically include a review of the literature (in journalism we say 'check the cuts' or 'cuttings'), gathering of documents and any available data, and interviews. The art of interviewing across a range of forms of journalism is beyond the scope of this dissertation. But it merits a brief mention because of its importance in conducting investigations.

In my view the 'pure' investigative journalistic interview should be open-ended, a trip to explore all avenues. Bell cites the renowned author on education research methods, Louis Cohen, referring to an analogy of an open-ended interview being like a fishing expedition. 'Like fishing, interviewing is an activity requiring careful preparation, much patience, and considerable practice if the reward is to be a worthwhile catch.' (Cohen, 1976, p.82). In his later book with Lawrence Manion, first published 1980, in a further analysis of interview methods, they describe four kinds of interview that might be used specifically as research tools: the structured interview; the unstructured interview; the non-directive interview and the focused interview. Each have their merits and are common to journalistic interviews – but the authors praise the unstructured interview as an open situation, having greater flexibility and freedom and although it is a more 'casual affair' it also has to be carefully planned (Cohen and Manion, 1994, p.273).

I have always been an advocate and practitioner of the more open-ended 'investigative' interview which necessarily takes time. It's a simple truth that you will find out more information, especially if you are trying to understand and analyse not just what the story is, but what the story is behind the story. (Hence I was far more suited to weekly and Sunday than to daily newspaper journalism.)

In the latter part of her accessible 'Guide for First-time Researchers' Bell explores the stages interpreting the evidence, reporting the findings and writing the report. I would argue that this is the social science equivalent of the later stages of IRASS – assimilation, structure and style.

In their book, *Research Methods in Education*, Cohen and Manion, the title of the introduction perfectly encapsulates my simple theory of the purpose of investigative journalism – 'The Nature of Inquiry: The Search for Truth'. In describing how people try to understand the world around them they say: 'The means by which they set out to achieve these ends may be classified into three broad categories: experience, reasoning and research.' The process of conducting a serious investigative inquiry also uses these elements.

Conduct of research

The general principle behind investigative journalism research is always to find things out, to try to get to the truth via interviews and original research. Loretta Tofani, a *Washington Post* Pulitzer prize-winner put it succinctly: 'You're trying to find out what is true.' (Ettema and Glasser, 1998). Or, as John Pilger said in a radio interview on BBC Radio Four's *Start the Week*, publicising his book *Tell Me No Lies* (1994) : 'Investigative journalism is about getting as close as you can – and only as close as you can – to truth-telling.'

In conducting my first two investigations for the *Independent on Sunday*, published in March and August 1990, into the evidence behind Satanic ritual abuse, I employed every principle I had learned and every skill I had acquired in my previous 13

My investigations into the myth

years as a reporter. It is important to remember that in 1990 there was no wide use of the internet, no Google, no email, no Facebook, no Twitter. The sources of research were Lexis Nexis for previous stories, telephone and face-to-face interviews and letters.

In the course of the four days research after the NSPCC press conference on Monday 12 March and the end of Friday 16 March (after which time it was rarely possibly to contact people), I began at the beginning. The beginning was the NSPCC press conference so I arranged a face-to-face interview with a press officer from the NSPCC at its headquarters in London.

The NSPCC had sent a questionnaire to its child protection teams in England, Wales and Northern Ireland (Scotland has the Royal Scottish Society for the Prevention of Cruelty to Children) and seven had reported they were working with children 'who are victims of ritualistic abuse'.

During the interview I wanted to establish: How did the NSPCC conduct its research? What questions did they ask in the questionnaire? Why did they embark on this research? Who were the sources which led to them conducting their research? Who do they recommend I speak to for further information about the wider picture?

The next stage was to pursue their sources and recommended contacts. Tellingly – although I didn't realise the significance of this at the time – the NSPCC referred me to the Evangelical Alliance (EA), which today says on its website it is the largest and oldest body representing the UK's two million evangelical Christians working across 79 denominations, 3,300 churches, 750 organisations and thousands of individual members. The EA is also a founding member of the World Evangelical Alliance, a global network of more than 600 million evangelical Christians. As I was later to discover, the worldwide evangelical Christian network proved to be the most powerful and effective influences in spreading the Satanic panic. The Evangelical Alliance put me in contact with other 'experts' who, in interviews, said they had personal experience of working with children and adult 'survivors' of ritual abuse.

These proved to be the chief 'claims-makers' in the UK. They included Maureen Davies of the Reachout Trust and Dianne Core, founder of Childwatch, who, as I reported as fact in the March 1990 story, said she had spoken to about 40 children from all over Britain who had suffered 'ritualistic' sexual abuse. I later discovered that in an interview with the American *New Federalist* newspaper in November 1988 (Burdman, 1988), at an international conference on Satanism in Rome in January 1989 she had claimed 4,000 children were sacrificed in Satanic rituals in Britain, each year. Core was also to play a crucial role in spreading the Satanic panic to Norway in 1991.

Another central character I interviewed for the March 1990 articles was the Rev Kevin Logan, vicar of St John's, Great Harwood, near Blackburn in Lancashire and author of *Paganism and the Occult* (1988), who gave me the most shocking and puzzling information of that week.

The more sensational stories that week included reports of 'confessions' of former Satanists talking of young girls being used as 'brood mares' – being made pregnant and having an abortion induced at five months so the foetus could be used in a sacrifice.' (Waterhouse, Kingman and Cuffe, 1990).

In the course of a long telephone interview. I asked the Rev Logan how many women or girls had told him personally that this had happened to them, and he said without hesitation, 'eight'. I was aghast. Eight. I was totally convinced this must be true. Why would a vicar lie?

Luckily I tape-recorded the telephone interview (as was my regular practice in complex investigations, for accuracy and in case of a dispute). Playing back the tape for my second investigation I belatedly realised the significance of what he said as background. What he told me was that these girls had 'confessed' to being members of Satanic cults and being used as 'brood mares' 'in the course of becoming Born Again Christians' (Cuneo, 2001, pp.195-198).

As I discovered, in the course of my second investigation, during that era there was a spate of books being written by people who had become Born Again Christians 'confessing' they had been a member of a Satanic cult and witness to and victim of depraved sexual acts. As I wrote in 'The Making of a Satanic Myth', the extraordinary spread of such stories can be traced to the publication in north America in 1980 (and in the UK in 1981) of *Michelle Remembers* (Smith and Pazder). During research for the second investigation I was referred to several such 'memoirs': *Delivered to Declare* by Gabrielle Trinkle and David Hall (1986); *Satan's Underground* by Lauren Stratford (1988); and *Dance with the Devil* by Audrey Harper and Harry Pugh, (1990) all published by Christian publishers. All these books have either been publicly debunked – *Michelle Remembers* by Nathan and Snedeker (1995), *Satan's Underground* by journalists working for the Christian magazine *Cornerstone* – or are patently fiction. The back covers give a flavour: 'At only six months Gabrielle Trinkle was tied to Satan by a blood bond.' 'Lauren Stratford … found herself part of a collection of young women and children forced to surrender their bodies in some of the most evil satanic rituals imaginable.' 'For years Audrey Harper carried a dark secret… She was the devil's dancing partner, and he wasn't going to let her go without a struggle.'

The fashion for 'misery memoirs' of this genre took off after the publication of *Sybil*, which purported to be the true story of horrendous physical and sexual (but not Satanic) abuse in childhood, memories of which were 'recovered when in therapy'. The book was spectacularly debunked by Nathan in *Sybil Exposed* (2011). So while I originally took as truth the Rev Logan's claim to have spoken personally to eight 'brood mares' I should have used reasoning and common sense and of course asked: What's the evidence?

Investigating 'The Making of a Satanic Myth'

Following publication of 'A Satanic Litany of Children's Suffering', Richard Williams, the editor of the prestigious *Independent on Sunday* Review, commissioned me to conduct a longer-term investigation to try to find out the truth about the NSPCC's allegations. I set out with no pre-conceived view about what I would find.

Jenny Cuffe sent me a fuller list of contacts, most of whom claimed to have encountered victims of ritual abuse by Satanic cults, including two social workers in Nottingham, several other social workers, paediatricians, a child psychiatrist, a detective chief superintendent and campaigners including Maureen Davies of the Reachout Trust, Audrey Harper (described in Cuffe's notes as a 'former witch'), the Rev Kevin Logan, and an Anglo-Catholic

Canon who was a member of a Christian Deliverance Study group. The list included Dr Fred Jonker, a GP who claimed he had encountered multiple cases of ritual child abuse by a Satanic cult in the town of Oude Pekela in the Netherlands. A Netherlands government inquiry concluded there was no evidence to substantiate this (Werkgroep Ritueel Misbruik, 1994).

Cuffe's list also included an academic from the London School of Economics, who studied new religious movements, who was sceptical, several occult bookshops and an organisation called ORCRO – Occult Response to Christian Response to the Occult – who 'countered' claims of Satanic ritual abuse. Following the first investigation in March 1990 I had received several letters which influenced the course of my next investigation. One was from the Pagan Federation, another from Chris Bray, the owner of an occult bookshop in Leeds, the Sorcerer's Apprentice. Both criticised the articles as credulous and inaccurate and urged me to investigate the evidence. They were speaking for occultists who argued they were being defamed by such stories. Bray wrote that he had amassed much research material about the origins and spread of the Satanic panic in the US, Canada and the UK, along with details of the main proponents of the stories if I would care to be enlightened.

I arranged to visit Bray at his shop. I was initially apprehensive: I had never knowingly met an occultist before. But he proved to an invaluable encyclopaedic source of information. Bray had compiled a chronology of local newspaper stories from the UK detailing the earliest stories sourced to a small group of people who were spreading the myth. Most of them were evangelical Christians.

Because of his bookshop business, much of which was mail order, Bray had an international network of people sending him newspaper cuttings about events in the UK and US related to the Satanic ritual abuse myth, as Bray called it. Bray pointed me to many sources in the UK and US, among them local newspaper articles from the late 1980s quoting two American visitors to the UK, Jerry Simandl and Sandi Gallant, warning about this new form of child abuse. They were both from a growing network of believers and proselytisers known as 'cult cops'. (Lanning, 1989; Hicks, 1989a, 1989b, 1990a, 1990b, 1991).

In the course of the investigation one interview led me on to others and I soon realised they fell into two polarised camps – with believers who were campaigners, therapists, social workers and 'survivors' on one side, and sceptics including criminal investigators and academics on the other. A self-proclaimed 'survivor', Sue Hutchinson, told a conference on incest which I attended in early August 1990 in Harrow, north-west London, that she had been a victim of ritual abuse for 16 years by Satanists and that human foetuses were being killed and eaten by 'Satanic sex rings'. She said that in the past six months she had dealt with 10 helpline calls a week from fellow survivors and that some of the 50 cases she was now counselling involved cannibalism. Vera Diamond, a Harley Street psychotherapist who co-organised the conference, said that several children had been killed during Satanic rituals and afterwards told me she had treated 20 adult survivors of ritual abuse. Norman Vaughton, a psychotherapist from Nottingham, said there were an estimated 10,000 human sacrifices a year in America, most of them 'foetuses that have been bred specially'.

Before that conference, in the course of my research, one case frequently cited as Satanic occurred in Nottingham where nine adults were convicted in a particularly abhorrent case of incest involving the sexual abuse of 23 children who had been taken into care.

As part of my methodology I decided to examine this case chronologically to see how and when the suggestion that this cases was 'Satanic' had first been introduced and by whom. During interviews with Christine Johnston and Judith Dawson, two of the social workers who believed the case involved a Satanic cult and animal and human sacrifice, they explained they had called in Ray Wyre, a former probation officer who then ran a clinic in Birmingham for sex offenders. I discovered that he had introduced to the case – and to foster mothers with whom the children were living – a list of 'Satanic indicators' – a profile of signs and symptoms to look for, which he had been given by Pamala Klein, an American social worker who was one of the earliest proponents of a belief in Satanic ritual abuse. The two social workers explained they had also contacted a consultant psychiatrist, secretary and founder of the Association of Christian Psychiatrists, who told me he counselled adult survivors of Satanic abuse and had organised a conference in March 1989 to warn of this new danger to children. At another conference in Reading in September 1989 the social workers first made public their belief that the Nottingham children had been victims of Satanic abuse. The police, finding no evidence, disagreed.

As I extended my enquiries beyond the UK and to the US, where the scare had evidently begun, I encountered sceptics who were adamant that despite dozens of forensic police investigations across the US, in Canada, the Netherlands and the UK, no corroborating evidence had been found.

As I wrote: 'They have produced no evidence. No bodies, no bones, no covens, no underground tunnels, no animal carcasses, no bloodstains. Nothing. Just the occasional court case where the pretence of supernatural powers was used to obtain silence and submission.'

The most convincing interviewees who led me into the 'no evidence' camp were Robert Hicks, an analyst with the criminal justice department in Virginia; Sherill Mulhern, an anthropologist from the University of Paris, who had studied self-declared Satanic abuse survivors and introduced me to the concept of multiple personality disorder and false memories 'recovered' in psychotherapy; and Kenneth Lanning of the National Centre for the Analysis of Violent Crime at the FBI Academy in Virginia.

In telephone interviews I asked each of them: If Satanic ritual abuse was a myth, how did it spread and cross the Atlantic to the UK?

Hicks, who had presented papers at conferences (Hicks, 1989a, 1989b), had written two sceptical articles (Hicks, 1990a, 1990b) and was writing a book on so-called Satanic cult crime (Hicks, 1991), blamed 'a loose network' of therapists, fundamentalist Christians, serving and ex-police officers and also the media for 'perpetuating the myth'. He told me: 'There were no such stories before the publication of *Michelle Remembers*.'

At the time I conducted a series of telephone interviews with her, Dr Mulhern was still conducting her pioneering research into the crossover between adult psychotherapists and child therapists reinforcing each other's beliefs. She later published a seminal chapter in a book (Mulhern, 1991) and a paper (Mulhern,

1994). She also gave two extended interviews, to a Christian magazine (1991) and to a radio station in New Zealand (1993). Her influence on my thinking was pivotal. She explained: '*Michelle Remembers* crystallised the Satanic abuse legend among psychotherapists. Adult therapists began networking with one another and with child therapists. I think the majority of adult survivors' accounts are the result of the interaction between the therapist, the patient and the surrounding Satanic cult stories.'

The turning point in my research that convinced me that Satanic ritual abuse did not exist was a paper presented at the FBI Academy in October 1989, reprinted from *The Police Chief* (Lanning, 1989), 'Satanic, Occult, Ritualistic Crime: A Law Enforcement Perspective'. I have the copy that was faxed over to me, marked all over, with asterisks, and highlighted in bright blue felt tip pen with comments from me including: 'definitive!'; 'quote at length, lessons for us all'; 'warning for UK'; and finally, 'quote in full, most sensible stuff I've read'.

In my article I quoted from his paper:

'The law enforcement perspective cannot ignore the lack of physical evidence. Until hard evidence is obtained and corroborated, the American people should not be frightened into believing that babies are being bred and eaten, and that 50,000 missing children are being murdered in human sacrifices. Satanic and occult crime has become a growth industry; speaking fees, books, videos, prevention material, television and radio appearances.'

PART 4

Theoretical interpretations

How my work relates to the theory and practice of investigative journalism

The role of other journalists in the Satanic panic

One of the most powerful and insightful reflections on the Satanic panic I found when researching this dissertation is by Margaret Talbot in the *New York Times Magazine*, 2001. Her analysis, with its controlled sense of outrage and injustice, so closely matches my own preoccupations and helps explain why I have kept pursuing the story even now, it merits an extract at length.

When you once believed something that now strikes you as absurd, even unhinged, it can be almost impossible to summon that feeling of credulity again. Maybe that is why it is easier for most of us to forget, rather than try to explain, the Satanic-abuse scare that gripped this country in the 1980s – the myth that Devil-worshippers had set up shop in our daycare centers, where their clever adepts were raping and sodomising children, practicing ritual sacrifice shedding their clothes, drinking blood and eating faeces, all unnoticed by parents, neighbors and the authorities.

Of course if you were one of the dozens of people prosecuted in these cases, one of those who spent years in jails and prisons on wildly implausible charges, one of those separated from your own children, forgetting would not be an option. You would spend the rest of your life wondering what hit you, what cleaved your life into the before and the after, the daylight and the nightmare. (Talbot, 2001)

Talbot was writing soon after the death, aged 74, of Peggy McMartin Buckey, one of the accused in the notorious McMartin preschool case.

'Believe the children' was the sanctified slogan of the moment – but what it came to mean, all too often, was believe them unless they say they were not abused. It didn't matter that no trace of the secret tunnels was ever found, that no physical evidence corroborated the charges (a black robe seized by the police as a Satanic get-up turned out to be Peggy's graduation gown), that none of the kiddie porn the abusers were supposedly manufacturing ever turned up, despite an extensive investigation by the F.B.I. and Interpol, that no parents who stopped by during the day ever noticed, say, the killing of a horse ...

The prosecution charged forward with a seven-year trial that became the longest and, at a cost of $15m, the most expensive criminal trial in American history. It resulted in not a single conviction, though seven people were charged in the McMartin case on a total of 135 counts – just a series of deadlocks, acquittals and mistrials. Buckey served two years in jail and her son Raymond served five. They spent their life's savings on lawyers' fees and in the end went 'through hell' and 'lost everything' as she put it after her 1990 acquittal. (Talbot, 2001)

'Believe the children' became the mantra of childcare professionals in the UK during our Satanic panic which followed a few years later and which was widely publicised after the NSPCC's press conference in March 1990. The mantra was recited again by childcare professionals, charities (including the NSPCC) and journalists during the crisis at the BBC in October/November 2012 over its flagship *Newsnight* programme, firstly for failing to broadcast an investigation into allegations of sexual abuse against the late BBC presenter Jimmy Savile, and then the disastrous broadcast of a story based on an interview with an alleged 'victim' falsely accusing a senior

Conservative – later erroneously identified as Lord McAlpine – of being involved in a paedophile ring sexually abusing boys in care homes in North Wales in the 1970s.

Interviewed on a BBC news programme at the height of the crisis, Mark Easton, home affairs editor, said what was most important in both these controversies, was that 'victims' should be encouraged to come forward, knowing they would be 'believed'.

This is wrong and dangerous. People alleging abuse should be listened to and their account rigorously tested for evidence.

What is investigative reporting?

In the introduction to a special issue of the *journal Journalism: Theory, Practice and Criticism* devoted to 'An International Symposium on Investigative Journalism' (2007), James Ettema and Theodore Glasser wrote: 'Investigative reporting can be journalism at its most politically vigorous and methodologically vigorous.'

Hugo de Burgh has a simple definition in the first edition of his book *Investigative Journalism: Context and Practice* (2000): 'An investigative journalist is a man or woman whose profession is to discover the truth and to identify lapses from it in whatever media may be available.'

A classic definition was coined by American investigative journalist Bob Greene in the foreword to the first edition of *The Reporter's Handbook: An Investigator's Guide to Documents and Techniques* produced by the American organisation Investigative Reporters and Editors (IRE), edited by John Ullmann and Steve Honeyman (1983):

It is the reporting, through one's own work product and initiative, matters of importance which some persons or organizations wish to keep secret. The three basic elements are that the investigations be the work of the reporter, not a report of an investigation made by someone else; that the subject of the story involves something of reasonable importance to the reader; and that others are attempting to hide these matters from the public (pp.vii-viii).

The origins of the term investigative reporter or journalist are unclear but the description seems to have entered the 'public lexicon', as O'Neill (2013) puts it, in the late 1950s and 1960s, significantly earlier than *All the President's Men*, the book of the Watergate scandal was published by Bernstein and Woodward in 1974. In his chapter in the book *Investigative Journalism: Dead or Alive?* (Mair and Keeble, 2011), Eamonn O'Neill quotes from an interview in 2006 with Green, then aged 77, saying he and other journalists were using the term in the late 1950s and 1960s.

Some journalists argue that all good journalism should be investigative. In an article in *British Journalism Review* in September 1998, Bruce Page, a member of the *Sunday Times* Insight team from 1964 to 1976, writes: 'Investigative technique is the foundation on which everything in journalism rests.' .

In his 1982 book *Interpretative Reporting* Curtis MacDougall writes:

The investigative reporter is like any other kind of reporter, only more so. More inquisitive, more sceptical, more resourceful and imaginative in knowing where to look for facts, more ingenious in circumventing obstacles, more indefatigable in the pursuit of facts and able to endure drudgery and discomfort (p.227).

In *The Universal Journalist* (2011), David Randall argues there are four distinguishing features required to justify the term investigative journalism: original research; the subject involves wrong-doing or negligence for which there is no published evidence; someone is trying to keep the information secret; and the stakes are high.

Alan Rusbridger, editor of the *Guardian*, draws a distinction between investigative and exposure journalism and gives his view on what constitutes the public interest. 'What's the public interest in a cricketer having a love romp in a hotel room or a rugby player having smoked cannabis 20 years ago? But if elected representatives are arguing a case in Parliament but not revealing that they are being paid to do so, then that strikes at the heart of democracy. That's public interest; this is an easy distinction.' (de Burgh, 2008, p.15)

De Burgh (2000) discusses the importance of a moral dimension of investigative journalism. He writes: 'To summarise, investigative journalists attempt to get at the truth where the truth is obscure because it suits others that it be so; they choose their topics from a sense of right and wrong which we can only call a moral sense; but in the manner of their research they attempt to be *dispassionately evidential.'* (My italics).

That is an important alternative phrase to objectivity. Until researching this dissertation I was convinced that I was firmly in the school of objective journalism – start with and an open mind, follow the facts and the evidence.

After following the story of the Satanic panic and the dangers of false memories of sexual, including Satanic abuse, being implanted by bad therapy, for more than 20 years, I think I have become less dispassionate and more angry as an individual and as a journalist about the damage caused by zealots who persist in the belief of the Satanic cult child sexual abuse conspiracy and the recovered memory therapy industry.

De Burgh suggests what motivates investigative journalists. 'They want to affect the way we see events or to make us care about something we have not thought about before; tell us what is and is not acceptable behaviour; champion the weak; accuse the guilty.' (2008, p.19).

He quotes Phillip Knightley in a 1999 interview on why he felt motivated to spend five years of his life on the thalidomide investigation: 'At first journalistic interest ... then, when I had met a victim, moral indignation, outrage ... at the sheer effrontery of men who could put pecuniary interest before their victims' lives.' (de Burgh, 2008, p.17)

Like Knightley, I began my investigation into the existence of Satanic ritual abuse out of journalistic interest. What was the evidence? During the course of the following 24 years investigating the Satanic ritual abuse myth and the recovered memory therapy industry, I also felt anger at lack of logic and common sense of so-called professionals promoting dubious theories and therapies, and latterly moral indignation at the injustice of false allegations.

I finally lost all 'dispassion' and objectivity when researching the background to the tragic case of Carol Felstead (alias Myers) for an article published in *Private Eye* in November 2011 which references a website set up by her family www.justiceforcarol.com. Carol died in 'mysterious circumstances', surrounded by medication, in 2005, after 20 years being treated by NHS and private psychiatrists and therapists who convinced her she was a victim of sexual abuse which never occurred by a Satanic cult which never existed (Waterhouse, 2011).

I believe the ideal for an investigative journalist is to be objective, or perhaps dispassionately evidential. But my own experience has shown me, there sometimes comes a point, when as a journalist you have crossed the line to moral indignation and outrage.

For essential reading on 'the journalism of outrage' and the concept of the investigative journalist as the 'custodian of conscience' (as Bethell, 1977, termed it), I turned to Ettema and Glasser (1988, 1989, 1998). Ettema's research monograph, *The Craft of the Investigative Journalist* (1988) summarises:

The Journalism of Outrage attempts to summon righteous indignation not merely at the individual tragedy but also at the moral disorder and social breakdown which the tragedy represents. Often, though not always, this form of journalism finds the blame for the suffering of innocent victims in the incompetence, indifference or illegal behaviour of public officials and agencies. And typically it demands, at least implicitly the response of the public and officials to the breakdown and disorder. This genre of journalism can, of course, be a force for social reform. But more fundamentally it is a ritual of moral commitment and renewal.

But, as Glasser and Ettema discuss in *Investigative Journalism and the Moral Order* (1989), the tension for investigative journalists, between 'righteous indignation' – a term they attribute to Ida Tarbell as 'an anthem to the muckrakers'- and custodians of conscience, and yet their idealised role as a 'detached observer of fact', has never been resolved.

Method

Bob Woodward has succinct advice for would-be investigative journalists in an interview published in *Investigative Journalism: Dead or Alive?* (Mair and Keeble, 2011). On the question 'Where do we get our information?' he describes three 'tracks': people, documents and (relating an anecdote from his editor early in his career) 'get your ass out of the chair and get over there'. This is particularly important in today's internet age when journalism students need to be prised away from their computer screens to go out and talk to people and observe for themselves.

In his book on investigative technique, Spark (1999) quotes several well known investigative journalists. John Ware, formerly *Panorama*, told him: 'Half the battle is looking at information and saying: What does this all mean? What are the key questions? The trick is knowing the right questions to ask. Once you're confident you know the right questions, you can try one way to get an answer and, if that's blocked, try another.'

TV programme maker Bernard Clark warns against assuming too readily that someone is crooked and dangerous and re-aligning the facts to support the case. 'You have to step back and say: 'Is what I'm doing here fair? It would be a better story doing it like this, but is it right?''

Spark quotes Christopher Hird advocating a classic methodology: '1. Get everything we can anywhere in the public domain (libraries, Companies House and so on). 2. Establish a chronology of events. We often see connections not seen before. 3. Relentlessly look up everybody who might know something.'

In December 2012 Hird became managing editor of the Bureau of Investigative Journalism, a non-for-profit venture based at City University London, to fund public interest investigative journalism. In talks to students on the MA in Investigative Journalism course at City University, in February and September 2013, Hird told students the process he followed in conducting investigations was 1) hypothesis; 2) analysis; and 3) synthesis. In his September talk he elaborated that many investigations begin with an 'evidential clue' which might lead to a hypothesis.

Hird recommends a handbook, *The Hidden Scenario: Plotting and Outlining Investigative Stories* by Luuk Sengers and Mark Lee Hunter (2012). This proposes that on beginning an investigation you start with a hypothesis, which then has to be interrogated. During the latter talk I questioned Hird about whether it was proper to begin with a hypothesis or, alternatively, an open mind. He argued a hypothesis was not a prejudice, not a closed mind, but, as with scientific method, you still need an open mind, you test the hypothesis and you need to be able to accept it might be wrong. In the case of my investigation into the Satanic abuse and false memory controversy, I most certainly began with an open mind. I wanted to know: What's the evidence for the existence of Satanic abuse? And later: What's the evidence for the validity of recovered memories? And later still: What's the evidence for the diagnosis of multiple personality disorder. It was only on the basis of my investigations that I developed hypotheses about each of these scenarios – that Satanic ritual abuse was a myth, recovered repressed memories were probably very rare and the diagnosis of MPD/DID was a professional 'fad' (McHugh, 1995, Frances and First, 1998, Paris, 2012, Frances, 2013, Waterhouse, 2013).

How my work relates to the academic literature in the field of psychology on false memories and multiple personalities

The 'memory wars'

In the worlds of psychiatry, psychology and psychotherapy the debate over whether people can recover long buried memories of traumatic events such as childhood sexual abuse or whether all or some such memories are false – encouraged by self-help manuals or 'implanted' by well-meaning but misguided therapists using questionable techniques – is polarised.

In 1999 Sapolsky wrote:

Lives have been destroyed over this incendiary issue – either those of the trauma victims (in one interpretation), left to wait decades for justice because of the workings of memory, or, in the counterview, those of the victims of false accusations, consumed in this season's witch-hunt. Civil war has nearly broken out among neuropsychologists over this issue, so let me tread lightly here – I will simply say that I have seen no scientific evidence for how such recovered memories might work, no supposed cases of it documented to be legitimate in a way that should satisfy a rigorous scientist, and plenty of scientific explanations for why various claims have not been legitimate. (Sapolsky 1999)

In 2003 Richard McNally wrote: 'How victims remember trauma is the most divisive issue is psychology today'.

In 2011 the 'civil war' was still raging. In reporting an online survey of therapists' experiences of, and beliefs about, recovered memories, Satanic abuse and dissociative identity disorder, James Ost et al. wrote:

The last 15 years have witnessed one of the most contentious debates in the history of psychology (Brainerd and Reyna, 2005). This debate, referred to by some as the 'memory wars' (Crews et al., 1995; McHugh, 2008), centred on the validity of claims made by adults that they had recovered memories of childhood sexual abuse that they had previously been unable to recall (Davies and Dalgleish, 2001; Geraerts et al. 2008; McNally, 2003).

While the majority opinion was that sexual abuse of children was more prevalent than had previously been thought, psychological opinion concerning the validity of claims based on recovered memories was divided on two key points. The first was whether individuals cope with traumatic experiences such as sexual abuse by blocking out conscious memory of the abuse (Brown et al. 1999, commentaries, McNally, 2003, Piper and Merskey, 2004, Piper et al. 2008). The second was whether certain therapeutic techniques might contribute to an individual developing a belief, or apparent memory, about having been sexually abused as a child when no such abuse had occurred. This was far from being a dry academic debate – the legal implications were and still are substantial. (Ost et al, 2011)

Advocates of the false memory position cite literature and studies by Elizabeth Loftus, famously the 'lost in the mall' studies (Loftus, 1993, Loftus and Pickerell, 1995) and Lindsay and Read (1994, 1995) on how misleading suggestions can distort memory. McNally (2003) concludes unequivocally that traumatic experiences are literally 'unforgettable'. A whole recovered memory movement – some might say industry – relies on literature supporting the theory that memories of extreme traumatic events can be suppressed and later recovered, Van der Kolk (1994), Shefflin and Brown (1996), Hammond et al (1998) Dalenberg (2006) . Notable critics of the studies of Loftus and Lindsay and Read include Pezdec (1994) Toon et al. (1996). Interestingly, an editorial in the *British Medical Journal* (1998) prefacing mention of the Sheflin and Brown study says: 'On critical examination, the scientific evidence for repression crumbles.'

Professional bodies are careful to tread a middle path. The American Psychological Association advises (2011) that experienced clinical psychologists state the phenomenon of a recovered memory is possible but rare and also that it is possible to construct pseudo-memories for events that never occurred. 'The mechanism(s) by which both of these phenomenon happen are not well understood and, at this point it is impossible, without other corroborative evidence, to distinguish a true memory from a false one.'

Research reviews: false memory

One of the earliest reviews of research on the 'false memory' debate, by Jacqui Farrants (1998), provides a thorough critique of the early, much-cited studies:

A long history of research on human memory documents the extent to which misleading suggestions can distort recall of events (Lindsay and Read, 1994). In a classic study, Loftus (1993) led five subjects to believe over a period, with the use of misleading and suggestive questioning, that a particular event occurred, for example that they had been lost in a shopping mall as a child. Loftus concluded that it is indeed possible to implant false memories that can be as vivid, internally coherent and detailed as true memories, and that repetition of the erroneous suggestions can lead to an acceptance by the subject of their truth. This she referred to as the 'misinformation effect' and Ceci and Loftus (1994) found such memory for non-events and the subjects' staunch belief in their reality to be far from rare. However this study is not without its critics.

It has been argued that studies such as these reveal nothing helpful to the study of memories of abuse. (Pezdek, 1994).

Caution needs to be exercised in generalising the Loftus study to other situations, as it has been criticised for manifold methodological flaws (Brown, 1995). Only five subjects took part in the experiment, all of whom were relatives or friends of the researcher, and no control subjects were used. This may introduce a confirmatory bias, something of which Loftus, herself, accuses memory recovery therapists. While the misinformation effect may provide some support for the notion that memory can be distorted through suggestive questioning, the extent to which entirely new memories can be created has been questioned ... Toon et al. (1996) dismiss the shopping mall study as irrelevant to the understanding of recovered abuse memories.

As Wright, Ost and French wrote in 2006, Loftus and Pickerell repeated the 'lost in the mall' study with a larger sample (1995), and other researchers showed that with a little encouragement (Ost, 2006), 'it was possible for participants to come to report relatively unusual events, events occurring in the first few days of life, medical procedures that never happened and negatively charged events ... The case studies we discuss later provide strong evidence that it is indeed possible to implant false memories of extremely traumatic events.'

One of the outcomes of research into false versus recovered memories is a landmark report, *Guidelines on Memory and the Law*, by the research board of the British Psychological Society, chaired by Martin A. Conway (2010). This sets out key points, which attempt to straddle the two camps of believers and sceptics:

Memories are records of people's experiences of events and are not a record of the events themselves. In this respect, they are unlike other recording media such as videos or audio recordings, to which they should not be compared.

Remembering is a constructive process. Memories are mental constructions that bring together different types of knowledge in an act of remembering. As a consequence, memory is prone to error and is easily influenced by the recall environment, including police interviews and cross examination in court.

Memories typically contain only a few highly specific details. Detailed recollection of the specific time and date of experiences is normally poor, as is highly specific information such as the precise recall of spoken conversations. As a general rule, a high degree of very specific detail in a long-term memory is unusual.

Recall of a single or several highly specific details does not guarantee that a memory is accurate or even that it actually occurred. In general the only way to establish the truth of a memory is with independent corroborating evidence. (p.2) .

In a more recent article, on being an expert witness, Conway argues that 'of course' there is no such thing as false memory 'syndrome', just a vast body of literature on how false memories can be created, (Conway, 2013).

And in a recent review of literature on false memories, in a collection of articles in the *Sage Handbook of Applied Memory* (2013), Newman and Garry write:

These studies tell us that memories are not an objective, unyielding imprint of the past, but a subjective, pliable patchwork of experiences, thoughts, and daydreams.

Studies have shown that Post-event information (PEI) [eg supplied by friends and trusted sources such as a therapist] is crafted to expose some people (but not others) to misleading suggestions about certain aspects of the event ... The finding that people incorporate inaccurate PEI into their memory reports is known as the misinformation effect (Loftus and Hoffman, 1989). Over the last four decades, hundreds of experiments conducted in laboratories all over the world have demonstrated that people often unwittingly adopt misleading suggestions as their own memories.

Considered as a whole, the vast misinformation effect literature shows that information we encounter after an event can invade us, as Loftus said, 'like a Trojan horse', precisely because we do not detect its influence (Loftus, 2007, p.4). It is the ease with which it hides in plain sight that makes it so dangerous, and its consequences so serious.

Recovered memories, multiple personalities, alien abductions and Satanic abuse.

Combining the concepts of recovered memories – including alien abductions and Satanic ritual abuse – and multiple personalities, Nicholas P. Spanos, Cheryl A. Burgess and Melissa Faith Burgess (1994) write:

People sometimes fantasise entire complex scenarios and later define these experiences as memories of actual events

Theoretical interpretations

rather than as imaginings. This article examines research associated with three such phenomena: past life experiences, UFO alien contact and abduction, and memory reports of childhood ritual Satanic abuse. In each case, elicitation of the fantasy events is frequently associated with hypnotic procedures and structured interviews which provide strong and repeated demands for the requisite experiences, and which then legitimate the experiences as 'real memories'. Research associated with these phenomena supports the hypothesis that recall is reconstructive and organised in terms of current expectations and beliefs... The large majority of patients who eventually receive a multiple personality disorder diagnosis do not display symptoms of multiplicity and are unaware that they have alter identities before entering treatment with the therapist who 'discovers' their multiplicity (Kluft, 1985). Moreover this 'discovery' frequently involves the use of highly leading hypnotic interviews in which patients are explicitly informed that they have alter personalities and attempts are made to communicate directly with these alters, learn their names, their functions, and so on ...

In their 2004 review of literature on multiple personality disorder, later redefined as dissociative identity disorder, 'The Persistence of Folly', Piper and Merskey write:

The literature shows that 1) there is no proof for the claim that DID results from childhood trauma; 2) the condition cannot be reliably diagnosed; 3) contrary to theory, DID cases in children are almost never reported; and 4) consistent evidence of blatant iatrogenesis appears in the practices of some of the disorder's proponents. Conclusions: DID is best understood as a culture-bound and often iatrogenic condition.

In their 'Review of Published Research on Adult Dissociative Identity Disorder from 2000-2010', published in January 2013, Guy Boysen and Alexandra VanBergen summarise the polarised arguments over whether DID is a valid psychiatric condition.

Fierce debate about DID emerged during the 1990s. Some individuals supported the veracity of DID as a post traumatic reaction to childhood abuse (David Gleaves, 1996), and others characterised DID as a culture-bound social phenomenon largely caused by treatment (Scott Lilienfeld et al., 1999; Nicholas Spanos, 1994); this controversy was never resolved. In fact there is currently a disagreement about DID's basic status as an accepted scientific concept. Some have argued that DID is a 'folly' that cannot be accepted scientifically because of lack of research (Piper and Merskey, 2004; Harrison Pope et al., 2006, Harrison Pope et al. 2007), while others argue that DID is an accepted and well-researched concept in the field of psychopathology.

In their latest paper (2012), Steven Lynn, Scott Lilienfeld and colleagues suggest a middle route.

We propose a perspective on dissociation based on a recently established link between a labile sleep-wake cycle and memory errors, cognitive failures, problems in attentional control, and difficulties in distinguishing fantasy from reality. We conclude that this perspective may help to reconcile the posttraumatic and socicocognitive models of dissociation and dissociative disorders.

From my research, the most prolific author of research and books as a proponent of belief in recovered memories, multiple personalities, Satanic ritual abuse and alien abduction is a Canadian psychiatrist, Dr Colin Ross (e.g. 1990, 1994, 1995, 1997, 2009).

Another long-time supporter of the concept of MPD and DID is David Spiegel (e.g. 1984, 1986, 1994, 2006, 2011), who successfully campaigned for DID to be retained in the fifth edition of the *Diagnostic and Statistical Manual of Mental Disorders*, *DSM-5* (American Psychiatric Association, 2013). In a 2011 paper Spiegel et al. wrote: 'There is a growing body of evidence linking the dissociative disorders to a trauma history, and to specific neural mechanisms.'

In an uncompromising criticism of the concept of DID and its inclusion in the *Dignostic and Statistical Manual*, arch-sceptic Joel Paris, a Canadian psychiatrist, wrote in late 2012:

DID, once considered rare, was frequently diagnosed in the 1980s and 1990s, after which interest declined. This is the trajectory of a medical fad. DID was based on poorly conceived theories and used potentially damaging treatment methods. The problem continues, given that the *DSM-5* includes DID and accords dissociative disorders a chapter in its manual ... DID is a psychiatric fad ... Only *DSM-5* has failed to notice that this diagnosis fails to meet criteria for a valid diagnosis. (Paris, 2012).

How my work relates to the academic literature in anomalistic psychology (the study of weird beliefs)

Anomalistic psychology is 'the psychology of weird experiences that people have and the beliefs that are associated with them' (French, interviewed by Waterhouse in the *Guardian*, 2008). It involves the study of how and why people believe things happened to them when there is no corroborating evidence. It is highly relevant to my investigations into Satanic abuse and also false memories and survivor stories (French and Stone, 2014, Grossman and French, 2010; French, 2008; Hood, 2009; McNally, 2003).

An extreme example is people who believe they have been abducted by aliens. I would place the phenomena of the Satanic ritual abuse myth and reported alien abduction in the same category – people who believe the unbelievable (Hood, 2009). In *Supersense: Why We Believe in the Unbelieveable*, Bruce Hood provides a refreshingly clear explanation for why, even within the same family, there can be believers and non-believers. He describes the distinction made by psychologists between the two processes of reasoning – intuitive and analytical.

According to Christopher French, professor of psychology and director of the Anomalistic Psychology Research Unit at Goldsmiths, University of London, and former editor of the *Skeptic* magazine, the position of the anomalistic psychologist and true sceptic remains – no evidence has been found to corroborate these stories, *so far.*

In the course of investigating the Satanic panic over the years I have tried to maintain this position. Journalists should be sceptical, but not cynical. As French stated in an interview with me, reported in the *Guardian* (2008): 'To be properly sceptical you have to be open to the possibility you might be wrong, and willing to be persuaded by evidence. Scepticism is not about dismissing claims before you look at the evidence. It's about saying, show me the evidence.'

So when relating my journalism to the anomalistic psychology of weird beliefs I have reflected on several questions: how can people believe they have been abducted by aliens? Or been sexually abused by Satanic cults? Or have 100 personalities?

Researchers have looked for answers in science – from neuro-science, in the study of the activities of the brain, to psychology and the phenomenon of 'sleep paralysis'; from the nature of memory to dubious methods of psychotherapy – involving hypnosis and drugs – implanting false memories.

Thalbourne's Australian sheep and goat scale of beliefs (2010) examines the psychological differences between people who believe in the paranormal (sheep) and those who don't (goats). Thalbourne was citing parapsychologist Gertrude Schmeidler, on her research into believers in extra-sensory perception (ESP), and she was citing Matthew 2:31-33 on judgment day.

In an early paper, Factors Underlying Belief in the Paranormal: Do sheep and goats think differently? (1992), French wrote: 'Even if paranormal forces do not exist, cognitive biases in human information processing would lead many people to believe they do ... the article examines the possibility that believers in the paranormal,(sheep), maybe more prone to them [cognitive biases] than disbelievers, (goats).'

In *Remembering Trauma* (2003), Richard McNally wrote (p.232) how the Harvard psychiatrist John Mack (1994) has reported, most of the 200 experiencers he studied recovered their memories of alien abduction while undergoing hypnosis or 'quasi-hypnotic procedures' designed to regress to moment of abduction. McNally wrote: 'The methods of helping people remember alien abduction are identical to those of recovered memory therapy.'

McNally and colleagues assessed 'alien abductees' who recovered memories with other clinicians. They found the typical abductee had a long standing interest in 'New Age' beliefs such as reincarnation, alternative healing, 'energy' therapies, telepathy, and astrology. Nearly all described themselves as being spiritual, though no longer practicing mainstream religion.

In a paper 'The Psychological Aspects of the Alien Abduction Experience' (Cortex, 2008), following a five-year study of 19 people in the UK who believed they were abductees, or had had encounters with extra-terrestrials, French concluded the 'experiencers' have a different psychological profile to people who did not claim to have had these experiences.

As I reported in the *Guardian* (Waterhouse, 2008), the research found experiencers have higher levels of paranormal belief, paranormal experience, self-reported psychic ability and fantasy proneness, more vivid imaginations, a greater tendency to hallucinate and more self-reported incidences of sleep paralysis. As I wrote: 'Sleep paralysis is a scientifically accepted condition. It usually happens between sleeping and waking, when the sufferer experiences a terrifying feeling of being paralysed, unable to move or speak, while an unidentifiable horror lurks in the dark. Six of the experiencers had undergone hypnotic regression, which French believes can implant false memories. Abductees showed higher levels of dissociativity (a tendency to switch off or have altered states of consciousness, such as out of body experiences and missing time episodes) and absorption (an ability to lose themselves in some activity such as watching a movie or reading a novel.'

Sleep paralysis as an explanation for the alien abduction experience is the theory put forward several researchers including Spanos (1993, cited by Susan Blackmore in 'Abduction by Aliens or Sleep Paralysis?', *Skeptical Inquirer*, 1998). She conducted research to test the findings of a poll by the Roper Organization in the US published in 1992. This claimed that 3.7 million Americans had certain 'indicator' experiences and therefore had probably been abducted by aliens. The paper, published privately and sent to nearly 100,000 psychiatrists, psychologists and other mental health professionals, was given added credibility in its introduction by John Mack, professor of psychiatry at Harvard Medical School, claiming hundreds of thousands of American men, women and children 'may' have experienced UFO abductions.

The figure of 3.7 million was an extrapolation based on 5,947 adults questioned about whether they had experienced certain events: 119 people (2 per cent) responded positively. Since the population represented by the sample was 185 million, the total number was 3.7 million. Experiences included leaving the body, flying through the air, seeing or dreaming of ghosts or UFOs, and waking up paralyzed with a sense of a strange person or presence in the room. In 'Abduction by Aliens or Sleep Paralysis?', Blackmore, reported that her study of 126 school children and 224 undergraduates, (in Bristol, UK), showed knowledge of aliens was related more to watching television than having the relevant experience. And, she concluded: 'I suggest that the best explanation for many abduction experiences is that they are elaborations of the experience of sleep paralysis.'

For other researchers, 'beliefs are not really about science.' (Clancy, 2005).

For her 2005 book, *Abducted: Why People Come to Believe They Were Kidnapped by Aliens*, Clancy conducted qualitative interviews with 'abductees', thinking rather more as an anthropologist than a psychologist.

"Pseudo-scientific' beliefs are proliferating because, for many people, science isn't working,' she wrote. Many people are on a quest to find truth and meaning. 'The stories we tell ourselves are ... a function of what we want to believe. Motivational and emotional considerations as well as intellectual factors are involved in the construction of autobiographical narratives.'

Newman and Baumesier (1996) suggest believers are seeking 'escape from ordinary self-awareness', rather like 'masochistic fantasies'.

Michael Shermer, in *Why People Believe Weird Things* (1997), has a simple but very compelling theory. 'More than any other, the reason people believe weird things is because they want to.' They might want immediate gratification, and go to a psychic; or for simplicity, morality and meaning they turn to God. Answering another question which has puzzled me he writes: 'Smart people believe weird things because they are skilled at defending beliefs they arrived at for non-scientific reasons.'

Smart in one field but not another. Why would a Harvard professor of psychiatry believe hundreds of thousands of Americans have been abducted by aliens? Perhaps because he has published research based on the research subjects he has hypnotised, saying they have? Or why would an expert in cognitive neuro-psychology, Professor John Morton, of the Institue of Cognitive Neuroscience, University College London, believe in self-proclaimed multiple personality 'survivor' Kim Noble's 20 personalities, as described in her 2011 memoir, *All of Me*, or the 100 fractured altered states as she told the *Guardian*, and endorse the rear cover of her book, describing her as the 'British gold standard for the extreme end of Dissociative Identity Disorder'? Perhaps, because, (according to Kim Noble's own website), she is one of his research subjects?

Shermer writes of theories, hypotheses, hunches, biases, prejudices amounting to 'confirmation bias'. 'We then sort through the body of data and select those most confirming what we already believe or ignore or rationalize away those that are disconfirming."

In an interview with the *Skeptic* volume 22, issue 3 by Kylie Sturgess, 'On the Origins of Supersense', Bruce Hood provides a compelling insight.

Whilst culture and indoctrination play a role, it can't be the entire explanation because even within the same family you can have believers and non-believers ... This might reflect a way that we rely on either our intuitive reasoning about the world or a more analytical, rational way of seeing the world. We have both ways of thinking – this is a typical distinction made by psychologists, we talk about the two processes of reasoning – one is intuitive and one is analytical.

The intuitive system probably operates very early in development, whereas the more rational, analytical system is one which comes much later in development and can be honed and fine-tuned through education. But within everyone there are two systems. The real difference between the believers and the non-believers is the extent to which the non-believers can suppress or inhibit the tendency to rely on intuition. But it never entirely goes away. (Sturgess, 2010).

For the extreme zealots – especially the mental health professionals and therapists – who continue to believe in the notions of Satanic ritual abuse, alien abduction and mind control, despite a total absence of corroborating evidence, I think other explanations are needed.

Will Storr, in his book *The Heretics: Adventures With the Enemies of Science* (2013), has concluded they have constructed a narrative, a story about themselves, in which they are heroes, and blinkered by 'confirmation bias'.

My evolving theory, first suggested to me by Michael Bromley, professor of international journalism at City University London, includes this: the bandwagon of believers displays the same defining features as a cult: secretive, paranoid, insular, seeking only confirmatory 'evidence'. And as I have struggled to understand why these people can continue to believe, I can also see the scenario of Clancy and Storr – the construction of narratives, in which they are the heroes, the likes of Valerie Sinason, Joan Coleman founder of the UK organisation Ritual Abuse Information, Network and Support and the Satanic abuse roadshow, battling the sceptics, like me.

Then some rather more human and base motives came to mind. Not to lose face. The historic zealots have staked their reputations on it. From Valerie Sinason in the UK, (Sinason, 1994, 2002), and the late Bennett G Braun and David Spiegel in the US, early contributor to book edited by Braun, *Treatment of Multiple Personality Disorder* (1986) and Spiegel, latterly main cheerleader for DID to remain in *DSM-5*, published in May 2013.

One of the most vociferous critics of DID as a valid diagnosis is Allen Frances, chairman of *DSM-IV*. In his book, *Essentials of Psychiatric Diagnosis*, published by the Guilford Press in May 2013, Frances writes: Fads in psychiatric diagnosis start with an exciting idea; a group of charismatic and gullible therapists then promotes it and a growing army of suggestible and theatrical patients dramatizes and spreads it.' Frances argues there was also a profit motive, that MPD became a "cottage industry' with weekend workshops turning out 'newly minted experts' on dissociation, creating increasing numbers of 'alters' or 'multiples' in patients in newly established long term and expensive inpatient units. 'The game was up when insurance companies stopped paying the bills.'

How my work relates to the academic literature on moral panics

Definitions

In *Moral Panics and the Media*, Chas Critcher writes:

It is agreed that moral panics are about morality, with the deviant groups or object constructed to enable a simplified dichotomy between good and evil ... it must involve a perceived threat to the moral order as a whole rather than a merely localised problem. It must ultimately cast this threat in the most basic terms of good and evil. Moral panics focus on inherent deviance which embodies evil, so threatening the moral order. (2003, p.144)

An historical perspective – and one particularly relevant to this dissertation – is given by Jeffrey S. Victor in *Moral Panics and the Social Construction of Deviant Behaviour: A Theory and its Application to the Case of Ritual Child Abuse* (1998):

The past offers numerous examples of collective behaviour during which widespread, fearful rumors and accusations about dangerous deviants resulted in false accusations of crime against many innocent people. Various terms have been used to label this form of collective behaviour: persecution, with-hunt, scare, and panic. The classic example is the European witch-hunt. (p.541)

Victor goes on:

How is it possible that a moral panic could be caused by widespread accusations of crime, lacking in evidence that the criminals even exist? The key insight is that accusations of crime are a claims-making activity. False accusations can construct imaginary deviants, when social control authorities systematically legitimise the accusations ... False accusations are a necessary part of a moral panic. (p.549).

Models of moral panic theory

In *Moral Panics and the Media* (2003), Critcher outlines two 'ideal types' of moral panic: one described by Stanley Cohen in *Folk Devils and Moral Panics* (1972), which he defines as a 'processual model', and the other elaborated by Erich Goode and Nachman Ben-Yehuda in *Moral Panics: The Social Construction of Deviance* (1994), which he describes as an 'attributional model'.

The opening paragraph of *Folk Devils and Moral Panics*, which identifies six stages of a moral panic, is justifiably famous among sociologists:

Societies appear to be subject, every now and then, to periods of moral panic. A condition, episode, person or groups of persons emerges to become defined as a threat to societal values and interests; its nature is presented in a stylised and stereotypical fashion by the mass media; the moral barricades are manned by editors, bishops, politicians and other right-thinking people; socially-accredited experts pronounce their diagnoses and solutions; ways of coping are evolved (or more often) resorted to; the condition then disappears, submerges or deteriorates and becomes more visible. (Cohen, 1972, p.9)

Theoretical interpretations

Goode and Ben-Yehuda are from a very different sociological tradition to Cohen that has generally been hostile to the concept of 'moral panic'. As Critcher writes:

In the USA, debates about the kinds of issues called moral panics in the UK have been dominated by a distinctive approach called social constructionism. Such work rarely cites the concept of moral panic. 'Scare' and 'panic' appear as descriptive term – even sometimes in the titles of major works – but they are not substantial concepts. (Critcher, 2003, p. 20)

Unusually, however, they believe that the concept has real worth:

Moral panics are differentiated from both social problems generally and specific moral crusades. Social problems differ from moral panics in lacking folk devils, panicky reactions or wild fluctuation of concern. Moral crusades are initiated by moral entrepreneurs, using the issue as a vehicle for their own interests. To become a moral panic, a crusade has to mobilise a wider constituency with a variety of interests. The crusade is an organised agitation, the moral panic a contingent alliance of interests. Such distinctions reveal the essential common characteristics of moral panics, five defining 'elements or criteria. (Goode and Ben Yehuda, 1994, p.33).

Criticher lists their five 'distinguishing attributes' of moral panics as '1. Concern; 2. Hostility; 3. Consensus; 4. Disproportionatilty; and 5. Volatility. Critcher asserts: 'The general case is that these five criteria must all be met for any case to be termed as a moral panic. This is in essence what we shall call *an attributional model of a moral panic*; cases lacking the attributes are not to be understood as moral panics.'

Satanic ritual abuse and moral panic

So did the international Satanic ritual abuse scares and interconnected recovered memory movement – bringing with it the epidemic of diagnoses of multiple personality disorder – amount to a moral panic?

Cohen, who died in 2013, thought it did. In his introduction to the third edition of *Folk Devils and Moral Panics*, in 2002, he wrote:

Another episode was more fictitious and one of the *purest* [my italics] cases of moral panic. Superimposed on the very real phenomenon of childhood sexual abuse and incest, came the 'recovered memory' of childhood incest: bitter debates about the existence of repressed (and recovered) memories of childhood sexual abuse. In these therapeutic interstices, came the story of 'ritual child abuse', 'cult child abuse' or 'Satanic abuse'. In around 1983, disturbing reports began circulating about children (as well as adults in therapy who were 'recovering' childhood memories) alleging they had been sexually abused as part of the ritual of secret, Satanic cults, which included torture, cannibalism and human sacrifice. Hundreds of women were 'breeders'; children had their genitals mutilated, were forced to eat faeces, were sacrificed to Satan, their bodies dismembered and fed to participants – who turned out to be family members, friends and neighbours, day-care providers and prominent members of the community. Claims-making for various parts of this story joined conservative Christian fundamentalists with feminist psychotherapists. (Cohen, 2002, p.xv)

A decade earlier (1992) Philip Jenkins and Daniel Maier-Katkin, took a similar position – 'the current concern about the occult appears to have all the hallmarks of a classic moral panic' – and the British-born sociologist Michael Hill (1998, 2005) concurs. Citing the publication of *Michelle Remembers* and the inclusion of MPD in the *DSM-III* Hill writes: 'In 1980, two books were published which produced the 'explosive amplification' that led directly to the moral panic.' (Hill, 2005) In footnote 15, he explains that the phrase 'explosive amplification' was first used by Gustav Henningsen in relation to the early modern witch hunts to characterise the 'temporary syncretism of the witch beliefs of the common people with those of the more specialised or educated classes', in *The Witches Advocate: Basque Witchcraft and the Spanish Inquisition* (Reno: University of Nevada Press, 1980, p391).

In her analysis of the American Satanic daycare centre scare, Mary deYoung (1998), clearly sees this as a moral panic, but argues that Cohen's classic moral panic theory needs to be updated to account for 'empowered folk devils' – the accused daycare workers and their supporters who fought the charges – and the views of society which were polarised into believers and sceptics. In her 1999 conference paper, 'The Devil Goes Abroad: The Export of the Ritual Abuse Moral Panic', deYoung states:

> Moral panic theory is in need of refinement. First, an updated theory must take into consideration the multi-mediated nature of the postmodern world that is the context of contemporary moral panics. The intricate web of relations between various interest groups, the nature of their sometimes contradictory discourse, and the international venues in which those claims are presented and contested must be part and parcel of moral panic theory. (deYoung, 1999)

Anthropologist Jean La Fontaine is perhaps the most authoritative and influential researcher to argue that moral panic theory alone does not account for what she terms the 'epidemic' of Satanic abuse allegations in the UK. In her 1998 book, *Speak of the Devil*, about her government-funded investigation into 84 alleged cases in the UK, La Fontaine argued there were more subtle but important forces at work, such as power struggles within the social work profession and later, within psychotherapy:

The extreme nature of the allegations in the case of Satanic abuse, and the absence of corroborative evidence to indicate that what was being alleged had actually happened, requires more explanation than the explanation in terms of moral panics can give it.

Fundamentalist tales of Satanic rituals draw on deep-seated cultural images of evil, that show continuity with the ideas underlying the witch-hunts of early modern Europe ... Further, the ideas are comparable (though not identical) to witch-beliefs in other parts of the world, described in this century. (La Fontaine, 1988, p.22)

In his analysis of whether the Satanic abuse scares in the US and the UK were moral panics Critcher (2003) reviews the research on the American daycare scare and seems to accept that the events did amount to a moral panic.

For Jenkins and Maier-Katkin (1992: 62) the Satanic scare consisted of a 'tissue of improbable charges' from 'unreliable witnesses' creating a 'classic moral panic'. Religious fundamentalist claims were endorsed by social work and mental health professionals, psychotherapists, lawyers and police officers. (Crichter, 2003, p.96).

Britain was different, however: 'Though the themes of child abuse were similar ... the events were not. American claims makers had more organisation, skills and credibility. The whole cultural climate seemed more susceptible to the acceptance of outrageous claims. Child abuse issues could therefore more easily assume the form of moral panics.' Critcher accepts that the American Satanic abuse panic spread: 'The clearest example of the USA exporting a ready-made panic was Satanic abuse.' (p.128). But he seems doubtful whether events in the UK fit the moral panic models, particularly regarding the role of the media. 'On ritual abuse, attempts to make claims and define the issue by quite disparate groups – Christian fundamentalists, social workers, pressure groups for children and some feminists – were summarily dismissed by the press.' (p.135)

This is at odds with my research findings. The chronology compiled by my early source Christopher Bray, the occult bookshop owner, reveals dozens of local newspaper stories starting in 1986 featuring anti-cult campaigners warning of the dangers of the occult. The first article to warn of Satanic child abuse was published in the Colchester *Evening Gazette*, in January 1988, featuring an interview with 'Satan's cop' Sandi Gallant from San Francisco police department – which I cited in a story in the *Independent on Sunday*, 16 September 1990, under the headline 'Satanic Cults: How the Hysteria Swept Britain' (Waterhouse, 1990d).

Moreover, in the immediate aftermath of the NSPCC briefing about Satanic ritual abuse in March 1990, the majority of the national media reported the claims as fact. It took almost six months before widespread scepticism set in. This was after my 'Making of a Satanic Myth' investigation in August 1990 and also after the Rochdale allegations of Satanic child abuse broke and police announced there was no evidence.

My research suggests that during the late 1980s and until late 1990, the Satanic abuse scare in the UK could indeed be seen as a moral panic. By ignoring this period and focusing on the later role of the media in attacking social workers rather than studying the origins of the Satanic abuse stories in the UK, sourced to the chief claims-makers, from 1986 up to autumn 1990, Criticher misses crucial evidence that fits the moral panic models of Cohen and Goode and Ben Yehuda.

Aftermath

After the La Fontaine report of 1994 found no evidence to substantiate the claims of Satanic abuse in the 84 allegations she investigated, all dating from between 1987 and 1992, the story faded away. But it resurfaced nearly a decade later, in 2003, when police charged nine adults of sexually abusing children on the Scottish island of Lewis.

After the arrests, the case was widely reported in the media as involving a paedophile ring. Because of my contacts, chiefly among groups of campaigners against false allegations, I was made aware that the allegations were in the context of Satanic rituals but that the police did not reveal this publicly, possibly because such claims had been discredited after the La Fontaine report in 1994.

When the case against the Lewis accused was thrown out by the Scottish Crown Office in July 2004 because of lack of evidence, I exclusively reported the Satanic abuse hidden agenda in a feature for the *Guardian*, 'It Was Like a Witch Hunt' (Waterhouse, 2004), and also acted as a consultant on a *Newsnight* film, timed to coincide with the *Guardian* feature.

I tried to discover how the Satanic panic returned. During an investigation for the *Daily Mail* (Barton and Waterhouse, 2005,) conducted with staff reporter Fiona Barton, working from interviews with some of the accused and on transcripts from the police interviews with one of the accused, we established that the allegations of Satanic rituals all originated from the mother of the three allegedly abused girls. It transpired the mother had epilepsy and learning difficulties and had herself been sexually abused by her father as a teenager. One accused man freely admitted to being a pagan. His paganism was a central focus of his police interviews. How and by whom the notion of Satanic abuse was introduced to the mother we never established. This remains a puzzle to me to this day. Was she in some sort of therapy? Was she a member of a church whose members believed in Satanic abuse?

In the US, there has been little media coverage of alleged Satanic ritual abuse, recovered memory, MPD/DID or related issues since the late 1990s, and as I wrote in my *New Scientist* feature (2013) the tenor of what coverage there has been has been sceptical following a series of multi-million dollar lawsuits against therapists brought by members of families falsely accused of sexual abuse and by former patients who have belatedly realised that they did not have multiple personalities and that their memories were false, implanted by the therapists.

In the UK, media interest has been sporadic, and most of it has been sceptical (Waterhouse, *Private Eye*, passim; Storr, 2011, 2013). In January 2013 a lead story in the *Sunday Express* in January 2013, suggested that the late Jimmy Savile (currently the subject of more than 450 allegations of sexual abuse dating back to the 1950s) was a Satanist and assaulted girls in Satanic rituals. The sole source of this 'Satanic Savile' story was Valerie Sinason, a Harley Street psychotherapist, one of the first claims-makers in the UK, who persists in promoting the notion of Satanic abuse, recovered memories and multiple personalities. I debunked the story in *Private Eye*, and none of the mainstream media picked it up (Waterhouse, *Eye*s, passim. notably Justice for Carol, Waterhouse, 2011; Devil woman 2012, Familiar Ritual, 2013). Scepticism about Satanic abuse is now almost universal in the UK media.

PART 5

Analysis of data evidence or outcomes

Since the outbreak of the international Satanic panic, numerous researchers and official inquiries have concluded there was no corroborating forensic evidence to substantiate the existence of Satanic ritual abuse. Outlining how tales of Satanic ritual abuse originated in the US and spread to Canada, the Netherlands, the UK, elsewhere in Europe and Australasia, deYoung (1999) writes:

What links these fantastic and far-flung vignettes is a moral panic about the Satanic ritual abuse of young children.... Its rapid dispersion was unimpeded by sundry international investigations that found no evidence to corroborate the allegations and warned that it is indeed a moral panic that is thrusting them into professional and public attention.

For an historical perspective of what remains today of the remnants of the Satanic panic, Philip Jenkins's *Intimate Enemies: Moral Panics in Contemporary Great Britain* (1992) offers a prophetic analysis.

Of the several panics outlined in this book, ritual abuse is the only one that can be said to have effectively ceased and to have been almost wholly discredited among media and policy makers. However, this does not mean that the concept itself has perished entirely. Some of the original claims-makers remain active, and the essential ideas of a ritualistic threat have been sufficiently publicised that they may well survive in the public consciousness until they re-emerge in some form as components of a future problem. (p.193)

Despite the continuing total absence of corroborating evidence, anywhere in the world, a minority of childcare professionals, including police officers, social workers, psychotherapists and counsellors, still persist to this day in the belief that Satanic ritual abuse exists.

Apart from the 2003 arrests on the Scottish island of Lewis (see above), the most prominent case was in Italy. In September 2011, five people including three female teachers from a school at Rignano Flaminio, outside Rome – two of them grandmothers

– were put on trial accused of sexually abusing, in the context of Satanic rituals, children as young as three. In May 2012, the first-instance judge acquitted all the defendants, ruling there was no case to answer. In November 2012 the judge issued the 'statement of grounds' for the acquittal of the five defendants which stated essentially that there is only circumstantial evidence ('prove indiziare') against them. The lawyer representing the parents of the allegedly abused children has said he will appeal.

In adult psychotherapy, psychology and psychiatry today a belief that adults can recover long buried 'repressed' memories of childhood sexual abuse, including Satanic ritual abuse, and that those patients sometimes suffer from dissociative identity disorder, formerly multiple personality disorder, persists among a minority of practitioners. Generally it is these people I have written about in my occasional series in *Private Eye* magazine under the headline 'Satanic Panic' (Waterhouse, *Eye*s passim).

A search of the internet using the terms ritual abuse and Satanic abuse brings up several organisations including RA-info.org, which lists dozens of conferences around the world; Ritual Abuse Network Scotland; safeline.org; endritualabuse.org. A book edited by James Randall Noblitt and Pamela Sue Perskin,

Ritual Abuse in the 21st Century (2008) features contributions from the most prominent claims-makers around the world.

The vast majority of academic researchers have long since concluded that Satanic ritual abuse is a myth. Official government funded reports following investigations in the US and UK, both published in 1994, established there was no corroborative evidence. (see La Fontaine, 1994; Goodman, Qin, Bottoms and Shaver, 1994).

As for the diagnosis of multiple personality disorder, now redefined as dissociative identity disorder, there still remains a hard core of believers. The latest version of the psychiatrists' handbook, the fifth edition of the *Diagnostic and Statistical Manual of Mental Disorders, DSM-5* (American Psychiatric Association, 2013), retains the diagnosis of DID.

But the overwhelming majority of researchers are sceptical about the validity of the MPD/DID diagnosis, and few who consider it valid in some circumstances believe the condition to be at all widespread.

Allen Frances and Michael First, respectively former chairman and editor of *DSM-IV*, wrote in their 1998 book: 'We do not deny altogether the existence of DID and together have seen what we believe to be three genuine cases in 45 collective years of practice. However, we are worried that the current over-diagnosis of multiple personality is an illusory fad that leads to misdiagnosis and mistreatment and does a disservice to the vast majority of patients who fall under its sway.'

The MPD diagnosis began to die out after a succession of successful multi-million dollar lawsuits against therapists in America brought by former patients who realised their memories were false. Many cases were fought by or co-ordinated by Dr Chris Barden, a lawyer and psychologist. As a result, the epidemic of MPD and DID was, if not halted in the US, slowed in its tracks.

Nevertheless, there is no room for complacency. In the UK there is a growing movement led by a Campaign for the Recognition and Inclusion of Dissociation and Multiplicity, launched in 2011, to have DID accepted as mainstream, the diagnosis accepted by NICE, the National Institute for Clinical Excellence, and for long-term funding of treatment by the National Health Service (Waterhouse, 2013b). In March 2013 the campaign held its second national meeting, in London, attended by around 200 'survivors' and therapists claiming to suffer from DID. According to a researcher I paid to 'go undercover' for the day, survivor stories included graphic accounts of Satanic abuse, alien abduction and mind control.

On balance, having read scores of academic papers and dozens of books on the concepts of repression, recovered memories and multiple personalities, and from my own investigations over more than 20 years, I am highly sceptical.

Two cases in particular have made indelible impressions on me and strengthened this scepticism. The first is the tragedy of Carol Felstead, who died in mysterious circumstances in 2005. From medical records obtained through the Freedom of Information Act, her family have pieced together evidence showing she suffered torment and became suicidal during 20 years in therapy where she recovered 'memories' and became convinced that she had been a member of a Satanic cult, with her parents the high priest and high priestess, and that she harboured multiple personalities, (Waterhouse, 2011). The second is a case I investigated for *New Scientist*, a Canadian woman we gave the pseudonym 'Carol', who recovered and later retracted memories she acquired in therapy – of being a victim and perpetrator of Satanic abuse, having been impregnated by an alien during a Satanic ritual and killed her child for sacrifice (Waterhouse, 2013b).

Analysis of data evidence or outcomes

As I told the audience at a talk in October 2013 at the Anomalistic Psychology Research Unit at Goldsmiths College, University of London, I am not a psychologist. I am a journalist and my job is to investigate and report the evidence, as we currently know it. As Chris French, director of this unit, has stressed, a true sceptic has to be prepared to be persuaded by evidence. To date I have seen no convincing evidence for the existence of Satanic ritual abuse, as classically defined by La Fontaine (1994).

In recent anonymous letters to *Private Eye*, in response to some of my articles, believers have cited three cases they claim to be 'evidence' for the existence of Satanic ritual abuse. In Germany in February 2002 Manuela and Daniel Ruda, described in court as 'self-styled devil worshippers', admitted the 'ritual Satanic killing' of a friend. They were ordered by the judge to be detained in a secure psychiatric unit.

In March 2011 Colin Batley, his estranged wife Elaine Batley, his lover, a prostitute, and another man described in court as a 'non-cult member' were convicted at Swansea crown court of a series of sexual assaults against children and young adults in the town of Kidwelly. The prosecution said Batley, also convicted of rape, was a 'self-styled high priest' of a 'quasi-religious' Egyptology-inspired occult cult.

At Truro crown court in December 2012, Peter Petrauske and Jack Kemp were convicted of sexual offences against children, in Petrauske's case including rape. The men were said to have donned robes and carried pagan paraphernalia. The prosecution said they 'used the cloak of paganism' to commit the offences but they were 'not pagans but child abusers'.

I am at the time of submission working on the Kidwelly case and hope to publish if it becomes possible. Meanwhile, in response to my *Private Eye* correspondents I cite La Fontaine's definition of ritual, not Satanic, abuse: 'These are cases where self-proclaimed mystical/magical powers were used to entrap children and impress them (and also adults) with a reason for the sexual abuse, keeping the victim compliant and ensuring their silence. In these cases the ritual was secondary to the sexual abuse which clearly formed the primary objective of their perpetrators.' (La Fontaine, 1994).

On the question of false memories, academics and clinicians from the worlds of psychiatry, psychology and psychotherapy remain polarised on the evidence for repression and recovered memories. For a reasoned overview on these I turn to researchers who are on the sceptical side of the fence, Wright, Ost and French (2006).

The argument is critical for the science of memory, but also for thousands of people who have either recovered memories or have been accused of abuse on the basis of such memories, not to mention the families and friends of all concerned. We believe: that what appear to be newly remembered (i.e. recovered) memories of past trauma are sometimes accurate, sometimes inaccurate, and sometimes a mixture of accuracy and inaccuracy; that much of what is recalled cannot be confirmed or disconfirmed; that because of these two beliefs, reports of past trauma based on such recovered memories are not reliable enough to be the sole basis for legal decisions.

PART 6

Critical appraisal of previous work

Responses to my work

I have appended critical appraisals from Jean La Fontaine, professor emeritus of social anthropology, London School of Economics, and Michael Hill, emeritus professor of Sociology, Victoria University of Wellington, New Zealand, who are familiar with my journalism.

I have also appended a list of citations of my journalism.

In one of the earliest citations and critiques of my 'thorough investigative reporting', Jeffrey S. Victor (1991) wrote:

In the fall and winter of 1990, a case of alleged ritual abuse created sensational newspaper stories in England, making headlines throughout that country. The case clearly illustrates the way that the collective behavior of the Satanic cult scare gives rise to witch hunts for ritual sex abusers of children.

However, after some more thorough investigative reporting, the attitude of the news reports and that of law enforcement agencies shifted toward concern about the parents and their children taken from them, perhaps unjustly by bureaucratic agents of government (*Waterhouse*, September 16, 1990; September 23, 1990; September 30, 1990; October 7, 1990) ...

The thorough investigative reporting of several newspapers, particularly *The Independent*, revealed the social dynamics which led to the creation of allegations of ritual abuse in Rochdale (*Waterhouse*, September 16, 1990; September 23, 1990; September 30, 1990; October 7, 1990). Initially, in 1988, several social workers with a Christian fundamentalist charity became concerned about ritual abuse after reading some American materials about the so-called 'signs' of ritual abuse. Some of them went to the US for training in how to identify ritual abuse. Later, back in England, they organised several conferences on the topic, which helped to popularise the Satanic cult conspiracy theory of ritual abuse. American 'experts' in ritual abuse were brought in as guest speakers, because the English social workers felt that the Americans were more informed about how to uncover these crimes ...

Critical appraisal of previous work

For a contemporary analysis of the Satanic panic, and my role as a journalist in questioning the evidence, I refer to a recent book, *The Myth of Moral Panics*, by criminologists Bill Thompson and Andy Williams, who describe how the media coverage of claims of Satanic abuse changed dramatically, from credulity to scepticism, particularly during the Orkney case in early 1991. They wrote:

The media set out to extricate itself from its uncritical coverage on the NSPCC's claims by pouring all over Orkney. This coverage bore no relationship to the standard horror-headlines. It was conducted by the UK's best journalists, such as Rosie Waterhouse and Barbara Jones, and they dug deep. The former, for example, uncovered that Orkney was not the first Scottish case, but was modelled on one in Ayrshire, where the parents had been jailed [*Independent* 14.4.1991]. No one had heard about it because of confidentiality clauses 'protecting' children from publicity (Waterhouse, 1991, 'The Secret Bungalow of Child Interrogation'; Thompson and Williams, 2013, p.194).

Conclusion

For a critical appraisal of my published work, I think, a concise overview of the journalism I submit for this PhD by prior publication, over the last 24 years, is: I dug deep. On reflection, I conclude that my investigations provide evidence for the concept of moral panics created through an 'explosive amplification' of anecdote, social and official concern about issues such as child abuse, spread by 'claims-makers' and a globalised mass media. Although sporadic claims of Satanic abuse continue I conclude there is still no corroborating evidence.

References

Acocella, J. (1998) 'The Politics of Hysteria', *New Yorker*, 6 April 1998, pp.64-79.

Alpert, J. L. (1996) *Working group on investigation of memories of childhood abuse: Final report*. American Psychological Association.

Alpert, J. L., Brown, L. S., Ceci, S. J., Courtois, C. A., Loftus, E. F. and Ornstein, P. A. (1998) 'Final conclusions of the American Psychological Association working group on investigation of memories of childhood abuse', *Psychology, Public Policy and Law*, 4(4), pp.933-940.

American Psychiatric Association (1980) *Diagnostic and Statistical Manual of Mental Disorders (DSM-III)*. Washington: American Psychiatric Publishing.

American Psychiatric Association (2013) *Diagnostic and Statistical Manual of Mental Disorders (DSM-5)*. Washington: American Psychiatric Publishing.

Aucoin, J.L. (2007) 'Journalistic Moral Engagement', *Journalism: Theory, Practice and Criticism,* 8(5), pp.559-572.

Barnett, J. and Hill, M. (1993) 'When the Devil Came to Christchurch', *Australian Religion Studies*, 6(2), pp.25-30.

Barton, F. and Waterhouse, R. (2005) 'The Accusations Couldn't Have Been More Lurid', *Daily Mail*, 2 March 2005.

Bass, E. and Davis, L. (1988) *The Courage to Heal*. New York: Harper and Row.

Bell, J. (2010) *Doing Your Research Project: A Guide for First Time Researchers in Education, Health and Social Science*. 5th edition. Maidenhead, Berkshire: Open University Press.

Bernstein, C. and Woodward, B. (1974) *All the President's Men*. New York: Simon and Schuster.

Best, J. (1990) *Threatened Children: Rhetoric and Concern about Child-Victims*. Chicago: University of Chicago Press.

Best, J. (ed) (2001) *How Claims Spread: Cross National Diffusion of Social Problems*. New York: Aldine de Gruyter.

Bethell, T. (1977) 'The Myth of an Adversary Press: Journalist as Bureaucrat', *Harper's Magazine*, January 1977, pp. 33-40.

Blackmore, S. (1998) 'Abduction by Aliens or Sleep Paralysis?', *Skeptical Inquirer*, 22(3), May/June 1998.

Bliss, E.L. (1980) 'Multiple Personalities: A Report of 14 Cases with Implications for Schizophrenia and Hysteria', *Archive of General Psychiatry*, 37(12), pp.1388-97.

Boysen, G.A. (2011) 'The Scientific Status of Childhood Dissociative Identity Disorder: A Review of Published Research', *Psychotherapy and Psychosomatics*, 80(6), pp.329-334.

Boysen, G.A. and VanBergen, A. (2013) 'A Review of Published Research on Adult Dissociative Identity Disorder 2000-2010', *The Journal of Nervous and Mental Diseases*, 201(1), pp.5-11.

Brainerd, C.J. and Reyna, V.F. (2005) *The Science of False Memory*. New York: Oxford University Press.

Braun, B.G. (ed) (1986) *The Treatment of Multiple Personality Disorder*. Washington: American Psychiatric Press.

British Medical Journal (1998) 'Editorial: Recovered Memories of Childhood Sexual Abuse', *British Medical Journal*, 316 (488), published 14 February 1998.

British Psychological Society (2010) *Guidelines on Memory and the Law. Recommendations from the Scientific Study of Human Memory. A Report from the Research Board*. British Psychological Society.

Brown, D. (1995) 'Pseudomemories: The Standard of Science and the Standard of Care in Trauma treatment', *American Journal of Clinical Hypnosis*, 37(3), pp.1-23.

References

Brown, D., Frischholz, E.J. and Scheflin, A.W. (1999) 'Iatrogenic Dissociative Identity Disorder – An Evaluation of the Scientific Evidence', *Journal of Psychiatry and Law*, 27(3-4), pp. 549-637.

Burdman, M. (1988) 'Childwatch Group Warns of Satanist Threat', *New Federalist*, 15 November 1998, p.4.

De Burgh, H. (ed) (2000) *Investigative Journalism: Context and Practice*. 1st edition. London: Routledge.

De Burgh, H. (ed) (2008) *Investigative Journalism: Context and Practice*. 2nd edition. London: Routledge.

Ceci, S.J. and Loftus, E.F. (1994) 'Memory Work': A Royal Road to False Memories?', *Applied Cognitive Psychology*, 8(4), pp.351-364.

Clancy, S.A. (2005) *Abducted: Why People Come to Believe They Were Kidnapped by Aliens*. Cambridge, MA: Harvard University Press.

Clapton,G.(1993) *The Satanic Abuse Controversy: Social Workers and the Social Work Press*. London: University of North London Press.

Cohen, L. (1976) *Educational Research in Classrooms and Schools: A Manual of Materials and Methods*. 4th edition. London: Routledge.

Cohen, L., Manion, L. (1994) *Research Methods in Education*. 4th edition. London: Routledge.

Cohen, S. (1972) *Folk Devils and Moral Panics: The Creation of the Mods and Rockers*. 1st edition. London: MacGibbon and Kee.

Cohen, S. (2002) *Folk Devils and Moral Panics*. 3rd edition. London: Routledge.

Conway, M.A. (2013) 'On Being a Memory Expert Witness: Three Cases', *Memory*, 21(5), pp.566-575.

Coons, P.M. (1986) 'The Prevalence of Multiple Personality Disorder', *Newsletter of the International Society for the Study of Multiple Personality and Dissociation*, 4, pp.6-8.

Core, D. (1989) Speech to Martin Luther King Rome Tribunal, panel on Satanism, 17 January 1989. Accessed by email from Chris Bray, Sub-culture Alternatives Freedom Foundation (SAFF) see yahoo email 9 November 2012.

Core, D. and Harrison, F. (1991) *Chasing Satan: An Investigation into Satanic Crimes Against Children.* London: Gunter Books.

Crews, F.C. (1995) *The Memory Wars: Freud's Legacy in Dispute*. New York: New York Review of Books.

Critcher, C. (2003) *Moral Panics and the Media*. Buckingham: Open University Press.

Cuffe, J. (1990) *Woman's Hour*, item on ritual child abuse, BBC Radio Four, 30 January 1990.

Cuneo, M.W. (2001) *American Exorcism: Expelling Demons in the Land of Plenty*. London: Bantam Books.

Dalenberg, C. (2006) 'Recovered Memory and the Daubert Criteria: Recovered Memory as Professionally Tested, Peer Reviewed, and Accepted in the Relevant Scientific Community', *Trauma Violence Abuse*, 7(4), pp. 274-310.

Davies, G.M. and Dalgleish, T. (eds) (2001) *Recovered Memories: Seeking the Middle Ground.* Chichester: John Wiley and Sons.

DeYoung, M. (1998) 'Another Look at Moral Panics: The Case of the Satanic Day Care Centres', *Deviant Behaviour*, 19(3), pp.257-278.

DeYoung, M. (1999) *'The Devil Goes Abroad': The Export of the Ritual Abuse Moral Panic.* Paper presented to the British Criminology Conference, Liverpool, July 1999. Published June 2000 and accessible at http://www.britsoccrim.org/volume3/004.pdf. Retrieved 8 August 2013.

DeYoung, M. (2004) *The Day Care Ritual Abuse Moral Panic*. Jefferson, North Carolina: McFarland.

Dyrendal, A. (2005) 'Media Constructions of "Satanism" in Norway (1988-1997)', *Skepsis* http://skepsis.no/?p=502

Ellis, B. (2000) *Raising the Devil: Satanism, New Religions, and the Media*. Kentucky: The University Press of Kentucky.

Ettema, J.S. (1988) *The Craft of the Investigative Journalist*. Evanston, Illinois: Northwestern University Institute for Modern Communications.

Ettema, J.S. and Glasser, T.L. (1988) 'Narrative Form and Moral Force: The Realization of Innocence and Guilt through Investigative Journalism', *Journal of Communication*, 38(3), pp.8-26.

Ettema, J.S. and Glasser, T.L. (1998) *Custodians of Conscience: Investigative Journalism and Public Virtue*. New York: Columbia University Press.

Ettema, J.S. and Glasser, T.L. (2007) 'Introduction: An International Symposium on Investigative Journalism, *Journalism: Theory, Practice and Criticism*, 8(5), pp.491-494.

Evans, H. (1983) *Good Times Bad Times*. London: Weidenfeld and Nicolson.

Farrants, J. (1998) 'The "False Memory" Debate: A Critical Review of the Research on Recovered Memories of Child Sexual Abuse', *Counselling Psychology Quarterly*, 11(3), pp.229-238.

Feldstein, M. (2007) 'Dummies and Ventriloquists: Models of How Sources Set the Investigative Agenda', *Journalism: Theory, Practice and Criticism*, 8(5), pp.491-494.

Finkelhor, D., Williams, L.M. and Burns, N. (1988) *Nursery Crimes: Sexual Abuse in Day Care*. Newbury Park: Sage Publications.

Frances, A. and First, M.B. (1998) *Your Mental Health: A Layman's Guide to the Psychiatrist's Bible.* New York: Scribner.

Frances, A. (2013) *Essentials of Psychiatric Diagnosis.* New York: Guilford Press.

French, C.C. (1992) 'Factors Underlying Belief in the Paranormal: Do Sheep and Goats Think Differently?', *The Psychologist*, 5, pp.295-299.

French, C.C., Santomauro, J., Hamilton, V., Fox, R. and Thalbourne, M.A. (2008) 'Psychological Aspects of the Alien Contact Experience', *Cortex,* 44, pp.1387-1395.

French, C.C. (2008) ' Weir or What?', *Guardian*, 14 October 2008.

French, C.C. (2009a) 'Families are Still Living the Nightmare of False Memories of Sexual Abuse', *Guardian,* 8 April 2009.

French, C.C. (2009b) 'Close Encounters of the Faked Kind,', *Guardian,* 9 November 2009.

French, C.C. (2013) quoted in 'The Woman with 48 Personalities' (Waterhouse, 2013b), *New Scientist*, 28 September 2013, pp46-49.

Geraerts, E., Bernstein, D.M., Merckelbach, H., Linders, C., Raymaekers, L., and Loftus, E.F. (2008) 'Lasting False Beliefs and their Behavioural Consequences', *Psychological Science*, 19(8), pp.749-753.

Glasser, T.L. and Ettema, J.S. (1989) 'Investigative Journalism and the Moral Order', *Critical Studies in Mass Communication*, 6(1), pp.1-20.

Gleaves, D.H. (1996) 'The Sociocognitive Model of Dissociative Identity Disorder: A Re-examination of the Evidence', *Psychological Bulletin*, 120(1), pp.42-59.

Goode, E.and Ben-Yehuda, N. (1994) *Moral Panics: The Social Construction of Deviance.* Oxford: Blackwells.

Goodman, G.S., Qin, J., Bottoms, B.L. and Shaver, P.R. (1994) *Characteristics and sources of Allegations of Ritualistic Child Abuse. Final Report to the National Center on Child Abuse and Neglect*. To cite: National Criminal Justice Reference Service http://www.ncjrs.gov.App/publications?abstract.aspx?ID=15441 5

Greene, R.W. (1983) in Ullmann, J. and Honeyman, S. (eds), *The Reporter's Handbook*. New York: St. Martin's Press.

Grossman, W.M., French C.C. (eds) (2010) *Why Statues Weep*. London: The Philosophy Press.

Guilliatt, R. (1996) *Talk of the Devil: Repressed Memory and the Ritual Abuse Witch-Hunt*. Melbourne: The Text Publishing Company.

Hammond, D.C. Brown, D.P. and Sheflin, A.W. (1998) *Memory, Trauma Treatment and the Law*. New York: W.W. Norton.

Harper, A.and Pugh, H. (1990) *Dance with the Devil*. Eastbourne: Kingsway Publications.

Harris, V. (1990) Letter to the editor, *Independent on Sunday*, 19 August 1990, p.17.

Henningsen, G. (1980a) *The Witches' Advocate: Basque Witchcraft and the Spanish Inquisition (1609-1614)* Reno, Nevada: University of Nevada Press.

Hicks, R. D. (1989a) *A Skeptical View of the Law Enforcement Approach*. Presentation at 11th Annual Crime Prevention Conference, Virginia Crime Prevention Association, Chesapeake, Virginia, 23 June 1989.

Hicks, R.D. (1989b) *None Dare Call it Reason: Kids, Cults and Common Sense*. Talk, Virginia Department for Children's 12th Annual Legislative Forum, Roanoke, Virginia, 22 September 1989.

Hicks, R.D. (1990a) 'Police Pursuit of Satanic Crime Part I', *Skeptical Enquirer*, 14, Spring 1990, pp.276-286.

Hicks, R.D. (1990b) 'Police Pursuit of Satanic Crime Part II', *Skeptical Enquirer*, 14, Summer 1990, pp.378-389.

Hicks, R.D. (1991) *In Pursuit of Satan: The Police and the Occult*. New York: Prometheus Books.

Hill, M. (1992) Review of *The Satanism Scare*, by James T Richardson, Joel Best and David Bromley, eds New York: Aldine de Gruyter, 1991, *Religion Today*, 7(2), pp.19-21.

Hill, M. and Barnett, J. (1994) 'Religion and Deviance' in Green. P. F. (ed), *Studies in New Zealand Social Problems*. 2nd edition. Palmerston North: Dunmore Press, pp231-249.

Hill, M. (1995a) 'Some Issues an Inquiry into the Civic Creche case could Examine', *Christchurch Press*, 31 March 1995.

Hill, M. (1995b) 'Satanic Ritual Abuse – Now You See it Now You Don't', *Australian Religion Studies*, 7(2), pp.58-64.

Hill, M. (1998) 'Satan's Excellent Adventure in the Antipodes', *Issues in Child Abuse Accusations*, 10, pp.112-121. Accessible at http:www.ipt-forensics.com/journal/volume10/j10_9.htm, retrieved 17 November 2013.

Hill, M. (2005) 'The "Satanism Scare" in New Zealand: the Christchurch Civic Creche Case', in Kirkman, Allison and Maloney, Duned (eds), *Sexualities in Aotearoa, New Zealand*. Otago University Press, 2005: pp 97-113.

Hill, M. (2008) 'When the Devil came to Christchurch', in Lews, J. and Peterson, J. (eds), *The Encyclopedic Sourcebook of Satanism*. Amherst, New York: Prometheus Books.

Holden, K.J. and French, C.C. (2002) 'Alien Abduction Experiences: Some Clues from Neuropsychology and Neuropsychiatry', *Cognitive Neuropsychiatry*, 7(3), pp. 163-178.

Hood, B.M. (2009) *Supersense: Why We Believe The Unbelievable*. New York: Harper Collins.

Jenkins, P. (1992) *Intimate Enemies: Moral Panics in Contemporary Great Britain*. New York: Aldine de Gruyter.

Jenkins, P. and Maier-Katkin D. (1992.) 'Satanism: Myth and Reality in a Contemporary Moral Panic', *Crime, Law and Social Change*, 17, pp.53-75.

JET Report, The Broxtowe Files (1990) http://www.users.globalnet.co.uk/~dlheb/jetrepor.htm rerieved 7 December 2013.

Kluft, R.P. (ed) (1985) *Childhood Antecedents of Multiple Personality*. Arlington, Virginia: American Psychiatric Association.

La Fontaine, J.S. (1994) *The Extent and Nature of Organised and Ritual Abuse: Research Findings*. London: HMSO.

La Fontaine, J.S. (1998) *Speak of the Devil: Tales of Satanic Abuse in Contemporary England*. Cambridge: Cambridge University Press.

Lanning, K.V. (1989a) *Satanic, Occult, Ritualistic Crime: A Law Enforcement Perspective*. Quantico, Virginia: National Centre for the Analysis of Violent Crime, FBI Academy. (Reprinted from *The Police Chief*, October 1989 58(10), pp.62-83.)

Lilienfeld, S.O., Kirsch, I., Sarbin, T.R., Lynn, S.J., Chavers, J.F., Ganawaya, G.K. and Powell, R.A. (1999) 'Dissociative Identity Disorder and the Sociocognitive Model: Recalling the Lessons of the Past', *Psychological Bulletin*, 125(5), pp.507-523.

Lilienfeld, S.O.; Lynn, S.J., Lohr, J.M. (eds) (2003) *Science and Pseudoscience in Clinical Psychology*. New York: The Guildford Press.

Lindsay, D.S. and Read, J.D. (1994) 'Psychotherapy and Memories of Childhood Sexual Abuse: A Cognitive Perspective, *Applied Cognitive Psychology*, 8(4), pp. 281-338.

Lindsay, D.S. and Read, J.D. (1995) '"Memory work" and Recovered Memories of Childhood Sexual Abuse: Scientific Evidence and Public, Professional and Personal Issues',

Psychology, Public Policy and the Law, 1(4), Special Issue: Witness Memory and the Law, pp.846-908.

Loftus, E.F. (1993) 'The Reality of Repressed Memories', *American Psychologist*, 48(5), pp. 518-537.

Loftus, E.F. (2007) 'Memory Distortions: Problems Solved and Unsolved', in Garry, M. and Hayne. H. (eds), *Do Justice and Let the Sky Fall: Elizabeth Loftus and her Contributions to Science, Law and Academic Freedom*. Hillsdale, New Jersey: Erlbaum, pp.1-14.

Loftus, E.F. and Hoffman, H.G. (1989) 'Misinformation and Memory: The Creation of Memory', *Journal of Experimental Psychology*, 118, pp.100-104.

Loftus, E.F. and Ketcham, K. (1994) *The Myth of Repressed Memory: False Memories and Allegations of Sexual Abuse*. New York: St Martin's Press.

Loftus, E.F. and Pickrell, J.E. (1995) 'The Formation of False Memories', *Psychiatric Annals*, 25(12), pp.720-725.

Logan, K. (1988) *Paganism and the Occult: A Manifesto for Christian Action*. Eastbourne: Kingsway Publications.

Lynn, J.S., Lilienfeld, S.O., Merckelbach, H., Giesbrecht, T. and van der Kloet, D. (2012) 'Dissociation and Dissociative Disorders: Challenging Conventional Wisdom', *Current Directions in Psychological Science*, 21(48), pp.48-53.

MacDougall, C.D. (1982) *Interpretative Reporting*. 8th edition. New York: Macmillan.

Mair,J. and Keeble, R.L. (eds) (2011) *Investigative Journalism: Dead or Alive?* Bury St Edmunds: Abramis Academic Publishing.

McHugh, P.R. (2008) *Try to Remember: Psychiatry's Clash over Meaning, Memory and Mind*. New York: Dana Press.

McNally, R.J. (2003) *Remembering Trauma*. Cambridge, MA: Harvard University Press.

References

Miraldi, R. (1990) *Muckraking and Objectivity: Journalism's Colliding Traditions*. Santa Barbara, California: Greenwood.

Mulhern, S. (1990) Quoted in 'The Making of a Satanic Myth', *Independent on Sunday*, 12 August, (Waterhouse 1990a).

Mulhern, S. (1991) 'Satanism and Psychotherapy: A Rumor in Search of an Inquisition', in Richardson, J.T., Best, J., Bromley, D.G.(1991), *The Satanism Scare*. New York: Aldine de Gruyter, pp.145-172.

Mulhern, S. (1994) 'Satanism, Ritual Abuse and Multiple Personality Disorder: A Sociohistorical Perspective', *International Journal of Clinical and Experimental Hypnosis*, 42(4), pp.265-288.

Nathan, D. (1990) 'The Ritual Sex Abuse Hoax', *Village Voice*, 12 January 1990.

Nathan, D. and Snedeker, M. (1995) *Satan's Silence: Ritual Abuse and the Making of a Modern Witch Hunt*. New York: Basic Books.

Nathan, D. (2011) *Sybil Exposed: The Extraordinary Story Behind the Famous Multiple Personality Case*. New York: Free Press.

Newman, E.J. and Garry, M. (2013) 'False Memory', in Perfect, T. J. and Lindsay, S. D. (eds), *The SAGE Handbook of Applied Memory*. New York: Sage Publications, pp. 110-126.

Newman, L.S., and Baumeister, R.F. (1996) 'Toward an Explanation of the UFO Abduction Phenomenon: Hypnotic Elaboration, Extraterrestrial Sadomasochism and Spurious Memories', *Psychological Inquiry*, 7(2), pp.99-126.

Nienhuys, J.W. (trans) (1994) *Report of the Working Group Ritual Abuse*, Ministry of Justice, The Hague, Netherlands.

Noble, K. with Hudson, J. (2011) *All of Me: My Incredible Story of How I Lived with the Many Personalities Sharing my Body*. London: Piatkus.

Noblitt, J.R., Perskin, P.S. (2000) *Cult and Ritual Abuse: Its History, Anthropology, and Recent Discovery in Contemporary America*. Westport, Connecticut: Praeger.

Noblitt, R. and Noblitt, P.P. (2008) *Ritual Abuse in the Twenty-First Century: Psychological, Forensic, Social and Political Considerations*. Bandon, Oregon: Robert D. Reed Publishers

O'Neill, E. (2011) 'Digging Deeper: Reflecting on the Development and Teaching of Investigative Journalism in a University Setting in the UK', in Mair, J. and Keeble, R.L.(eds) *Investigative Journalism: Dead or Alive?* Bury St Edmunds: Abramis Academic Publishing.

Ost, J. (2006) 'Recovered Memories', in Williamson, T. (ed) *Investigative Interviewing: Rights, Research, Regulation*. Devon: Willan Publishing, pp.259-291.

Ost, J., Wright, D., Easton, S., Hope, L. and French, C. (2011) 'Recovered Memories, Satanic Abuse, Dissociative Identity Disorder and False Memories in the UK: A Survey of Clinical Psychologists', *Psychology, Crime and Law*, 17, pp.1-19.

Page, B. (1998) 'A Defence of "Low" Journalism', *British Journalism Review*, 9(1), pp.45-58.

Paris, J. (2012) 'The Rise and Fall of Dissociative Identity Disorder', *Journal of Nervous and Mental Disease*, 200(12), pp.1076-1079.

Pazder, L. (1981) *Michelle Remembers: New Frontiers in Psychiatry*. Evening panel, 134th annual meeting of the American Psychiatric Association, New Orleans, 9-15 May, moderator Lawrence H. Pazder; participant Michelle D. Smith.

Pezdek, K. (1994) 'The Illusion of Illusory Memory', *Applied Cognitive Psychology*, 8(4), pp.339-350.

Pilger, J. (ed) (2004) *Tell Me No Lies: Investigative Journalism and Its Triumphs*. London: Jonathan Cape.

Piper, A. and Merskey, H. (2004) 'The Persistence of Folly: A Critical Examination of Dissociative Identity Disorder. Part 1. The Excesses of an Improbable Concept', *Canadian Journal of Psychiatry*, 49(9), pp.592-600.

Piper, A., Lillevik, L. and Kritzer, R. (2008) 'What's Wrong with Believing in Repression?: A Review for Legal Professionals', *Psychology, Public Policy and Law*, 14(3), pp.223-242.

Pope Jr., H.G., Barry, S., Bodkin, A. and Hudson, J.I. (2006) 'Tracking Scientific Interest in the Dissociative Disorders: A Study of Scientific Publication Output 1984-2003', *Psychotherapy and Psychosomatics*, 75(1), pp.19-24.

Pope Jr., H.G., Poliakoff, M.B., Parker, M.P., Boynes, M. and Hudson, J.I. (2007) 'Is Dissociative Amnesia a Culture-bound Syndrome? Findings from a Survey of Historical Literature', *Psychological Medicine*, 37(2), pp.225-234.

Randall, D. (2011) *The Universal Journalist*. 4th edition. London: Pluto Press.

Richardson, J.T., Best, J. and Bromley, D.G.(1991) *The Satanism Scare*. New York: Walter de Gruyter.

Richardson, J.T. (1997) 'The Social Construction of Satanism: Understanding an international Social Problem', *Australian Journal of Social Issues*, 32, pp.61-86.

Richardson, J.T. (2003) 'Satanism and Witchcraft: Social Construction of a Melded but Mistaken Identity', in Davis, D. H. and Hamkins, B., *New Religious Movements and Religious Liberty in America*. Texas: Baylor University Press, p. 199.

Richardson, James T., Reichert and J., Lykes, V. (2009) 'Satanism in America: An Update', *Social Compass*, 56(4), pp.552-563.

Ross, C.A. (1997) *Multiple Personality Disorder: Diagnosis, Clinical Features and Treatment*. New York: John Wiley.

Ross, C.A., Miller, S.D., Reagor, P., Bjornson, L., Fraser, G.A. and Anderson, G. (1990) 'Structured Interview data on 102 Cases of Multiple Personality Disorder From Four Centers', *American Journal of Psychiatry*, 147(5), pp.596-601.

Ross, C.A. (1994) *The Osiris Complex: Case Studies in Multiple Personality Disorder*. Toronto: University of Toronto Press.

Ross, C.A. (1995) *Satanic Ritual Abuse: Principles of Treatment*. Toronto: University of Toronto Press.

Ross, C.A. (1997) *Dissociative Identity Disorder: Diagnosis, Clinical Features and Treatment of Multiple Personality*. New York: John Wiley.

Ross, C.A. (2009) 'Errors of Logic and Scholarship Concerning Dissociative Identity Disorder', *Journal of Child Sexual Abuse*, 18(2), pp.221-231.

Rossen, B. (1989) 'Mass Hysteria in Oude Pekela', *Issues in Child Abuse Accusations*, 1, pp.49-51.

Sapolsky, R.M. (1999) 'Stress and Your Shrinking Brain: Post Traumatic Stress Disorder's Effect on the Brain', *Discover*, 20(3), pp.116-122.

Schreiber. F. R. (1973) *Sybil: The True Story of a Woman Possessed by Sixteen Separate Personalities*. Chicago: Henry Regnery Company.

Sengers, L. and Hunter, M.L. (2012) *The Hidden Scenario: Plotting and Outlining Investigative Stories*. London: Centre for Investigative Journalism.

Sheflin, A.W. and Brown, D. (1996) 'Repressed Memory or Dissociative Amnesia: What the Science Says', *Journal of Psychiatry and Law*, 24, pp.143-88.

Shermer, M. (1997) *Why People Believe Weird Things: Pseudoscience, Superstition and other Confusions of our Time*. New York: Henry Holt and Company.

Showalter, E. (1997) *Hystories: Hysterical Epidemics and Modern Media*. London: Picador.

Sinason, V. (ed) (1994) *Treating Survivors of Satanist Abuse*. London: Routledge.

Sinason, V. (2002) *Attachment, Trauma and Multiplicity: Working with Dissociative Identity Disorder*. London: Routledge.

Smith, M. and Pazder, L. (1980) *Michelle Remembers*. New York: Congdon and Lattes.

Spanos, N.P., Weekes, J.R. and Bertrand, L.D. (1985) 'Multiple Personality: A Social Psychological Perspective', *Journal of Abnormal Psychology*, 94(3), pp.362-376.

Spanos, N.P., Cross, P.A., Dickson, K. and DuBreuil, S.C. (1993) 'Close Encounters: An Examination of UFO Experiences, *Journal of Abnormal Psychology*, 102(4), pp.624-632.

Spanos, N.P. (1994a) 'Multiple Identity Enactments and Multiple Personality Disorder: A Sociocognitive Perspective', American Psychological Association *Psychological Bulletin*, 116(1), pp.143-165.

Spanos, N.P., Burgess, C.A., and Burgess M.F. (1994) 'Past-life Identities, UFO Abductions and Satanic Ritual Abuse: The Social Construction of Memories', *International Journal of Clinical and Experimental Hypnosis*, 42(4), pp.433-446.

Spanos, N.P. (1994b) 'Multiple Identity Enactments and Multiple Personality Disorder: A Sociocognitive Perspective', *Psychological Bulletin*, American Psychological Association 116(1):143-165

Spanos, N.P. (1996) *Multiple Identities and False Memories: A Sociocognitive Perspective.* Washington, DC: American Psychological Association.

Spark, D. (1999) *Investigative Reporting: A Study in Technique*. Oxford: Focal Press.

Spiegel, D. (1984) 'Multiple Personality as a Post-traumatic Stress Disorder. *Psychiatric Clinics of North America*, 7(1), pp.101-110.

Spiegel, D. (1986) 'Dissociation, Double Blinds, and Posttraumatic Stress in Multiple Personality Disorder', in Braun, B. (ed), *Treatment of Multiple Personality Disorder*. Washington: American Psychiatric Press.

Spiegel, D. and Scheflin, A. W. (1994) 'Dissociated or Fabricated? Psychiatric Aspects of Repressed memory in Criminal and Civil Cases', *International Journal of Clinical and Experimental Hypnosis,* 42(4), pp.411-432.

Spiegel, D., (2006) 'Editorial: Recognizing Traumatic Dissociation', *American Journal of Psychiatry*, 163, pp.566-568.

Spiegel, D., Loewenstein, M.D., Lewis-Fernandez, R., Sar, V., Simeion, D., Vermetten, E., Cardena, E. and Dell, P.F. (2011) 'Dissociative Disorders in DSM-5', *Depression and Anxiety*, 28, pp.824-852.

Storr, W. (2011) 'The Mystery of Carol Myers', *Observer*, 11 December 2011.

Storr, W. (2013) *The Heretics: Adventures with the Enemies of Science*. London: Picador.

Stotter, M. (2012???) 'Simon Hall – Introducing the TV Detective: Interview with Simon Hall, BBC TV Crime Correspondent', Shots Crime and Thriller Ezine, date???. Accessible at www.shotsmag.co.uk/feature_view.aspx?FEATURE_ID=66, retrieved 12 December 2013.

Stratford, L. (1988) *Satan's Underground: The Extraordinary Story of One Woman's Escape.* Eugene, Oregon: Harvest House Publishers.

Sturgess, K. (2010) 'The *Skeptic* Interview with Bruce Hood: On the Origins of Supersense', *The Skeptic*, 22(3):, pp.27-30.

Summit, R.C. (1983) 'The Child Sexual Abuse Accommodation Syndrome', *Child Abuse and Neglect,* 7, pp.177-193.

Talbot, M. (2001) 'The Devil in the Nursery', *New York Times Magazine*, 7 January 2001. Accessible from the *New America Foundation* http://newamerica.net/node/6298, retrieved 23 November 2012.

Taylor, W.S., Martin, M.F. (1944) 'Multiple Personality', *Journal of Abnormal and Social Psychology*, 39(3), pp.281-300.

Thalbourne, M.A. (2010) 'The Australian Sheep-Goat Scale: Development and Empirical Findings', *Australian Journal of Parapsychology*, 10(1), pp.5-39.

Thigpen, C.H. and Cleckley, H.M. (1954) 'A Case of Multiple Personality', *Journal of Abnormal and Social Psychology*, 49(1), pp.135-151.

Thigpen, C.H. and Cleckley, H.M. (1957) *The Three Faces of Eve*. New York: McGraw-Hill.

Thigpen, C.H. and Cleckley, H.M. (1984) 'On the Incidence of Multiple Personality Disorder: A Brief Communication', *International Journal of Clinical and Experimental Hypnosis*, 32(2), pp.63-66.

Thompson, B. and Williams, A. (2013) *The Myth of Moral Panics: Sex, Snuff and Satan*. Abingdon, Oxford: Routledge, p.194.

Thompson, K. (1998) *Moral Panics*. London: Routledge.

Tighe, C. (1988) 'Children Sexually Abused in Satanic Rituals, says Group', *Daily Telegraph*, 14 March 1988, p.3.

Todd, R. (1990) 'Kids forced Into Satan Orgies,' *Daily Mirror*, 13 March 1990, pp.1-2.

Tofani, L. (1998) 'Introduction: The Reporter's Craft as Moral Discourse', in Ettema, J.S. and Glasser, T.L. (1998), *Custodians of*

Conscience: Investigative Journalism and Public Virtue. New York, Columbia University Press.

Trinkle, G. and Hall, D. (1986) *Delivered to Declare.* London: Hodder and Stoughton..

Ullmann, J. and Honeyman, S. (eds) (1983) *The Reporter's Handbook: An Investigator's Guide to Documents and Techniques.* New York: St Martin's Press.

Van der Kolk, B.A. and Van der Hart, O. (1989) 'Pierre Janet and the Breakdown of Adaptation in Psychological Trauma', *American Journal of Psychiatry*, 146, pp.1330-1342.

Van der Kolk, B. A. (1994) 'The Body Keeps the Score: Memory and the Evolving Psychobiology of Posttraumatic Stress', *Harvard Review of Psychiatry*, 1(5), pp.253-265.

Victor, J.S. (1990a) 'Satanic Cult Rumors and Contemporary Legend', *Western Folklore*, 49(1), pp.51-81.

Victor, J.S. (1990b) 'The Spread of Satanic-Cult Rumors', *Skeptical Inquirer*, 14(3), pp.287-291.

Victor, J. S. (1991) 'The Satanic Cult Scare and Allegations of Ritual Child Abuse', *Issues in Child Abuse Accusations*, 3, pp.135-43.

Victor, J.S. (1992) 'Ritual Abuse and the Moral Crusade against Satanism', *Journal of Psychology and Theology*, 20(3), pp.248-253.

Victor, J.S. (1993) *Satanic Panic: The Creation of a Contemporary Legend.* 1st edition. Chicago: Open Court.

Victor, J.S. (1993) 'Sexual Attitudes in the Contemporary Legend about Satanic Cults', *Issues in Child Abuse Accusations*, 5, pp.83-8.

Victor, J.S. (1994) 'Fundamentalist Religion and the Moral Crusade Against Satanism: The Social Construction of Deviant Behavior', *Deviant Behavior*, 15(3), pp.305-334.

References

Victor, J.S. (1996) *Satanic Panic: The Creation of a Contemporary Legend.* 4th edition. Chicago: Open Court.

Victor, J.S. (1998) 'Moral Panics and the Social Construction of Deviant Behaviour: A Theory and Application to the Case of Ritual Child Abuse', *Sociological Perspectives*, 41(3), pp.541-565.

Walker, I., Quinn, J. and Day, P. (1990) 'Analysis: The Attack on Innocence; Venom has Driven Social Workers and Police Apart', *Mail on Sunday*, October 1990.

Waterhouse, R., Kingman, S. and Cuffe, J. (1990) 'A Satanic Litany of Children's Suffering', *Independent on Sunday*, 18 March, p.5.

Waterhouse, R. (1990a) 'The Making of a Satanic Myth', *Independent on Sunday*, 12 August 1990, p.8.

Waterhouse, R. (1990b) 'Victims of Satanic Cult Myth Need Care, Say Psychiatrists', *Independent on Sunday,* 19 August 1990.

Waterhouse, R. (1990c) 'Death of a Satanic Myth', *Daily Mail*, 15 September 1990.

Waterhouse, R. (1990d) 'Satanic Cults: How the Hysteria Swept Britain', *Independent on Sunday*, 16 September 1990

Waterhouse, R. (1990e) 'Children's Games that Bred Alarm over "Satanism"', *Independent on Sunday*, 23 September 1990.

Waterhouse, R. (1990f) 'NSPCC Faces Sack over "Satanic" Abuse Role', *Independent on Sunday*, 23 September 1990.

Waterhouse, R. (1990g) 'NSPCC Questions Led to Satan Cases', *Independent on Sunday,* 30 September 1990.

Waterhouse, R. (1990h) 'Satanic Inquisitors from the Town Hall', *Independent on Sunday,* 7 October 1990.

Waterhouse, R. (1990i) 'Police Chief to 'Kill Off' Abuse Stories', *Independent on Sunday*, 7 October 1990.

Waterhouse, R. (1990j) Ritual abuse dismissed by police', *Independent on Sunday,* 4 November 1990.

Waterhouse, R. (1991) 'The Secret Bungalow of Child Interrogation', *Independent on Sunday,* 14 April 1991

Waterhouse, R. (1992) 'A Modern Witch Hunt', *The Oldie*, 21 February 1992.

Waterhouse, R. (1993a) 'Parents' Group Fights 'False' Sex Abuse Claims', *Independent*, 11 May 1993.

Waterhouse, R. (1993b) 'Families Haunted by Accusations of Childhood Abuse', *Independent*, 24 May 1993.

Waterhouse, R. (1994a) 'Government Inquiry Decides Satanic Abuse Does Not Exist', *Independent on Sunday*, 24 April 1994.

Waterhouse, R. and Strickland, S. (1994) 'Abuses of Memory', *Independent on Sunday*, 1 May 1994.

Waterhouse, R. (1994) 'Satanic Abuse Dismissed as a Myth by Government Inquiry', *The Independent,* 3 June 1994.

Waterhouse, R. (1994) 'There'll be the Devil to Pay', *Independent*, 17 October 1994.

Waterhouse, R. (1998) 'New Witch Hunters', *Mail on Sunday*, 1 February 1998.

Waterhouse, R. (2004) 'It was Like a Witch Hunt', *Guardian*, 16 July 2004.

Waterhouse, R. (2004b) (consultant) 'A Case of Satanic Panic', *BBC Newsnight*, 16 July.

Waterhouse, R. (2006a) 'Satanic Panic: "The Appalling Damage Done to Children"', *Private Eye* 1150, January 20, 2006.

Waterhouse, R. (2006b) 'Satanic Panic: A Can of Worms', *Private Eye* 1153, March 3, 2006.

Waterhouse, R. (2008) 'Weird ... or What?', *The Guardian* October 14, 2008.

Waterhouse, R. (2011) 'Satanic Panic: Justice for Carol', *Private Eye* 1302, November 25, 2011.

Waterhouse, R. (2012) 'Satanic Panic: Devil Woman', *Private Eye* 1325, October 18, 2012.

Waterhouse, R. (2013a) 'Satanic Panic: Familiar ritual', *Private Eye* 1334, February 22, 2013.

Waterhouse, R. (2013b) 'The Woman who had 48 Personalities', *New Scientist*, 28 September, 2013 pp.46-49.

Waterhouse, R. (2013c) *Satanic Abuse, False Memories and Multiple Personalities: Anatomy of a 23 year Investigation*. Presentation, Anomalistic Psychology Research Unit, Goldsmiths College, University of London, 29 October.

Werkgroep Ritueel Misbruik (1994) *Rapport van Werkgroep Ritueel Misbruik (Report of the Ritual Abuse Workgroup)* The Hague: Ministrie van Justite.

Wilby, P. (2012) 'The importance of finding things out', Email, 24 November.

Wright, D.B.; Ost, J. and French, C.C. (2006) 'Recovered and false memories', *The Psychologist*, 19(6), pp.352-355.

Appendix 1: Critical appraisals

a. Jean La Fontaine

Rosie Waterhouse is an impressive journalist. Her method of work is finding out the facts behind any issue and her conclusions are demonstrably based on the evidence in an unusually scientific manner. She was, I think, the only journalist in Britain who, when she found out that allegations about the Satanic abuse of children that were sweeping the country in the late 1980s and early 1990s were not supported by evidence, had the courage to go against the majority of her colleagues and make this public. Her article 'The Making of a Satanic Myth' was original, factual, extremely well argued and preceded the publication of my more academic research which came to similar conclusions. Her work thus added considerably to the public's knowledge about moral panics and the mechanics of construction of public fantasy.

The investigation that led her to this conclusion was by any academic standard, thorough and rigorous. In pursuing connected issues of 'recovered memories' and 'multiple personality disorder' subsequently she has not altered her commitment to empirical research and careful analysis. This is of considerable importance in a period where much academic

Appendix 1: Critical appraisals

writing is of a speculative and introspective nature, largely abandoning the commitment of science to the elucidation of data. As the motto of London School of Economics has it, the academy aims ' to seek the causes of things'.

In recent years Rosie has been almost the only journalist to keep alive the serious doubts about 'recovered memories' until support is beginning to be given her by authoritative work on the issue by academics. More to the point, the work is being given publicity which it might not have obtained had the controversy not been kept alive by her series in *Private Eye*. She has consistently reminded the public that allegations are not evidence and that additional proof and explanation must be offered before an allegation should be accepted as a true record.

Rosie Waterhouse has undoubtedly contributed to knowledge in more than one discipline and her conclusions advance sociological and psychological understanding. Few Ph.D.s can claim more, some not as much.

J.S. La Fontaine, B.A. Ph D. (Cantab.), (Hon)Ph.D. Linkoping, Ph.D.(Univ) Open University, D.Litt (Hon) Goldsmiths, London

Professor Emeritus of Social Anthropology, London School of Economics

b. Mike Hill

The scholarly journalism of Rosie Waterhouse is of the finest standard and provides a robust and reliable examination of an area fraught with heated controversy. I can personally attest to the contribution which her work has made to my own research on the 'Satanism scare' as it migrated to Australia and New Zealand. Her first newspaper and magazine articles in the early 1990s presented an impressively argued and evidence-based response to many of the wild but widely accepted claims about the alleged satanic abuse of children and in doing so succeeded in injecting a note of sanity into the debate. She was tackling a moral panic which had erupted in North America in the 1980s, spread to the UK a few years later, and reached the Antipodes in the late 80s and early 90s. Though the prevailing response to such satanic claims is at the present time one of scepticism, it must be strongly emphasised that when her initial investigative articles appeared the context was significantly different, with support for the Satanism scenario pervasive in both print and visual media. It is no exaggeration to state that Rosie's contribution was one of the major contributors to this change in public attitudes.

In 1990, when my research interest in the Satanism scare was initially developing, there was considerable ambivalence in

New Zealand about the validity of the claims being made. It should be noted that newspapers in New Zealand syndicate material from international sources, principally UK newspapers. In Wellington there were two daily papers, the *Dominion*, a morning paper, and the *Evening Post*. Depending on the syndicated source, there was confusion about the Satanism coverage, which regularly appeared because of the involvement of a New Zealand Presbyterian minister in a prominent episode in the Orkneys. The morning paper tended to reprint articles from sources such as the *Observer*, which at the time was somewhat 'soft' on satanic claims; while the evening paper would rely on the *Independent* as its principal source. The latter's scepticism, which was evidenced in Rosie's contributions, was patently more evidence-based and, to a sociologist whose research specialisms were religion and deviance, its accounts were considerably more plausible. However, it was only when I embarked on eight months of research leave in London in the latter part of 1991 that I came to appreciate fully the importance of her work in the *Independent* and the *Oldie*. The insightfulness of her sceptical conclusions was further confirmed in discussions with Jean La Fontaine, who was currently writing a report for the British government on the Satanic claims, and in the publication of James Richardson et al.'s *The Satanism Scare*, which I reviewed. In retrospect, Rosie was an important influence on the subsequent direction of my own research.

Over a decade later, her impressive pioneering investigation of the Satanism scare, and her continued monitoring of its current derivatives in *Private Eye*, can be more comprehensively appreciated. Investigative journalism of this quality requires a skilled substratum of well assimilated conceptual knowledge. To the literature on moral panics should be added a cluster of psychological constructs including recovered memory and multiple personality. Rosie shows a thorough grasp of this material and this enables her to subject the empirical material to analytical scrutiny. The psychological literature is voluminous and frequently controversial; thus it is a measure of her scholarship that she has developed a proficiency in so much of it.

To conclude on a personal level, when I returned to New Zealand after my leave in mid-1992, I was soon confronted by a local Satanic moral panic which was focussed on a crèche in Christchurch. There were a number of strident claimsmakers and at the time scepticism was very much a minority, and frankly lonely position. But with the background awareness I had gathered in the UK, and with Rosie's articles to provide support, it was possible to maintain a sceptical stance with greater confidence. As in the UK, this scepticism is now widely held. So I have particular reason to value her journalistic achievement and to commend its embodiment in a PhD.

Michael Hill, BA (Soc), PhD (Lond)

Emeritus Professor of Sociology, Victoria University of Wellington, New Zealand

(Formerly Lecturer in Sociology, London School of Economics 1967-75, and Visiting Professor, National University of Singapore, 1996-97 and 2007-2010)

Appendix 2: Citations of published journalism

Citations of my journalism relevant to the PhD by Prior Publication.

a. Articles

Ahrens, J. G. (1995) 'Recovered Memories: True or False-A Look at False Memory Syndrome'. *University of Louisville Journal of Family Law*, 34, p.379.

Bauman, Z. (1998) 'On Postmodern Uses of Sex', *Theory, Culture & Society*, 15(3), pp.19-33.

Doig, A. (1992) 'Retreat of the Investigators', *British Journalism Review*, 3(4), pp.44-50.

Gallagher, B. (2001) 'Assessment and Intervention in Cases of Suspected Ritual Child Sexual Abuse', *Child Abuse Review*, 10(4), pp.227-242.

Hannabuss, S. and Allard, M. (1994) 'Issues of Religious Censorship', *Library Review*, 43(8), pp.14-30.

Hewson, B. (2003) 'Fetishing Images', *Spiked-online*, 23 January 2003. Accessible at: http://www.spiked-online.com/Printable/00000006DC06.htm, retrieved 2 December 2013. [Citing 'The Making of a Satanic Myth'.]

Hill, M. (1998) 'Satan's Excellent Adventure in the Antipodes', *Issues in Child Abuse Accusations*, 10, pp.112-121.

Money, J. (1992) 'Semen-Conservation Theory vs. Semen-Investment Theory, Antisexualism, and the Return of Freud's Seduction Theory', *Journal of Psychology and Human Sexuality*, 4(4), pp.31-45.

Parker, H., Gallagher, B., and Hughes, B. (1996) 'The Policing of Child Sexual Abuse in England and Wales', *Policing and Society: An International Journal*, 6(1), pp.1-13.

Pratt, J. (2005) 'Child Sexual Abuse: Purity and Danger in an Age of Anxiety', *Crime, Law and Social Change*, 43(4-5), pp.263-287.

Victor, J. S. (1991) 'The Satanic Cult Scare and Allegations of Ritual Child Abuse', *Issues in Child Abuse Accusations*, 3, pp.135-43. [Citing four articles from 1990, including 'The Making of a Satanic Myth' and 'Satanic Cults: How the Hysteria Swept Britain'.]

Victor, J.S. (1992) 'Ritual Abuse and the Moral Crusade Against Satanism', *Journal of Psychology and Theology*, 20(3), pp.248-253. [Citing four articles from 1990.]

Victor, J. S. (1994) 'Fundamentalist Religion and the Moral Crusade against Satanism: The Social Construction of Deviant Behavior', *Deviant Behavior*, 15(3), pp.305-334.

b. Books

Aburish, S. K. (2012) *The Rise, Corruption and Coming Fall of the House of Saud: With an Updated Preface*. London: Bloomsbury Publishing.

Bauman, Z. (2013) *The Individualized Society*. Hoboken, New Jersey: Wiley, p.235.

Bennett, G. (2009) *Sex, Violence and Disease in Contemporary Legend*. Mississippi: University Press of Mississippi, pp.1, 3, 6, 8. [Citing five articles including 'The Making of a Satanic Myth'.]

Bolton, R. (1990) *Death on the Rock and Other Stories*. London: WH Allen, pp.290-292.

DeYoung, M. (2004) *The Day Care Ritual Abuse Moral Panic*. Jefferson, North Carolina: McFarland, pp.168, 236.

Itzin, C. (ed) (2000) *Home Truths about Child Sexual Abuse: Policy and Practice*. Abingdon: Oxford: Routledge.

Jenkins, P. (1992) *Intimate Enemies: Moral Panics in Contemporary Great Britain*. New York: Aldine de Gruyter, pp.179, 188, 251 [Citing five articles from 1990-91.]

La Fontaine, J.S. (1998) *Speak of the Devil: Tales of Satanic Abuse in Contemporary England*. Cambridge: Cambridge University Press, pp.5, 171, 193.

Pilger, J. (1994) *Distant Voices*. London: Vintage, pp.184, 434.

Pilger, J. (1998) *Hidden Agendas*. London: Vintage, p.457.

Sikes, P. and Piper, H. (2009) *Researching Sex and Lies in the Classroom: Allegations of Sexual Misconduct in Schools*. Abingdon, Oxford: Routledge, p.14. [Citing 'The Making of a Satanic Myth'.]

Tate, T. (1991) *Children for The Devil*. London: Methuen, pp.57, 58, 334-335.

Thompson, B., Williams, A. (2013) *The Myth of Moral Panics: Sex, Snuff and Satan*. Abingdon, Oxford: Routledge, p.194.

Victor, J.S. (1996) *Satanic Panic: The Creation of a Contemporary Legend*. Peru, Illinois: Open Court, pp.122, 324.

Webster, R. (2005) *The Secret of Bryn Estyn: The Making of a Modern Witch Hunt*. Oxford: The Orwell Press, pp.xvi, 88, 448, n122.

Appendix 3: List of published and broadcast journalism submitted as my body of published work

The following is a list of publications of Rosie Waterhouse relevant to the submission for PhD by prior publication. It also includes a list of television, radio and film contribution and lists of relevant talks and presentations and professional memberships.

Note that articles marked with a single asterisk (*) have not been submitted. For articles in *Private Eye*, which are anonymous, see email from Ian Hislop, the editor, confirming that I am the author.

a. Published articles

'A Satanic Litany of Children's Suffering: Sexual perversion, animal sacrifice and the drinking of blood are among the bizarre rituals adding a shocking new dimension to abuse of the young. Co-authors Rosie Waterhouse, Sharon Kingman and Jenny Cuffe on the evidence behind this week's NSPCC report.' *Independent on Sunday*, p.5, 1,158 words, 18 March 1990.

'The Making of a Satanic Myth: Adult"survivors" tell horrific tales of ritual child abuse but the evidence is missing', *Independent on Sunday*, p.8, 2,205 words, 12 August 1990.

'Victims of Satanic Cult Myth Need Care, say psychiatrists', *Independent on Sunday*, p.2, 883 words, 19 August 1990.

Appendix 3: List of published and broadcast journalism submitted as my body of published work

'Death of a Satanic Myth: Is there a single shred of real evidence to show a cult of devil worship?' (Edited version of *IoS* piece, 'The Making of a Satanic Myth', copyright *Independent on Sunday*) *Daily Mail*, p.6, 1,500 words, 15 September 1990.

'Satanic Cults: How the Hysteria Swept Britain. Child abuse – or occult rituals? Rosie Waterhouse traces the events leading to trauma for Rochdale families', *Independent on Sunday*, p.3, 1,473 words, 16 September 1990.

'Children's Games that Bred Alarm over 'Satanism': Rosie Waterhouse examines how cases in Nottinghamshire led to hysteria about "ritual abuse"', *Independent on Sunday*, p.6, 1,115 words, 23 September 1990.

'NSPCC Faces Sack over 'Satanic' Abuse Role', *Independent on Sunday*, p.1, 402 words, 23 September 1990.

'NSPCC Questions led to Satan Cases', *Independent on Sunday*, p.8, 932 words, 30 September 1990.

'Satanic Inquisitors from the Town Hall', *Independent on Sunday*, p.6, 2,276 words, 7 October 1990.

'Police Chief to "Kill Off" Abuse Stories', *Independent on Sunday*, p.1, 349 words, 7 October 1990.

'Evangelists Campaign Against Hallowe'en', *Independent on Sunday*, p.3, 816 words, 21 October 1990.

'Witch-hunt is Launched Over Books and TV' (co-authored with Sarah Strickland), *Independent on Sunday*, p.3, 1,169 words, 28 October 1990.

'Ritual Abuse Dismissed by Police', *Independent on Sunday*, p.2, 272 words, 4 November 1990.

'Hungry for Souls: The evangelicals are on the march – out of the church, down the corridors of power and onto the air waves. But is their fervour bring with it a dangerous intolerance? A special investigation by Rosie Waterhouse with Sarah Strickland', *Independent on Sunday* Review, cover story, pp.3-6, 3,500 words, 13 January 1991.

'Judge Dismisses Status of Satanic Abuse "Therapist', *Independent on Sunday*, p.3, 1,067 words, 24 March 1991.

'Therapist's Role in Notts Case', *Independent on Sunday*, p.3, 585 words, 7 April 1991.

'The Secret Bungalow of Child Interrogation. Rosie Waterhouse traces the events in Ayrshire, where 10 children were seized in a similar nightmare to the cases in Orkney', *Independent on Sunday*, p.4, 1,333 words, 14 April 1991.

'New Satanic Abuse Case Collapses', *Independent on Sunday*, p.1, 545 words, 26 May 1991.

'The Ritual Abuse of Children and Young People: Myth, fact, fiction or reality?' *Private Eye*, Church News, 400 words, 19 July 1991.*

'Sex Claims "Destroyed Family"', *Independent*, 800 words, 11 August 1991.

'Witch Hunt. Children for the Devil: Ritual abuse and Satanic crime', *New Statesman and Society*, p.36, book review, 800 words, 6 September 1991.

'"Therapist" Linked to Epping Case', *Independent*, 350 words, 1 December 1991.

'Police in National 'Satanic Abuse' Survey', *Independent*, p.6, 420 words, 5 January 1992.

Appendix 3: List of published and broadcast journalism submitted as my body of published work

'A Modern Witch Hunt: Satanic abuse rears its ugly head again this week. But despite a vociferous campaign on both sides of the Atlantic there is still no evidence that it exists. Rosie Waterhouse investigates', *The Oldie*, launch issue, pp.10-13, 3,000 words, 21 February 1992.

'Satanic Video Shows Art, Not Abuse', *Independent on Sunday*, p.2, 801 words, 23 February 1992.

'Legal Threat to Channel 4 over "Satanic" Woman', *Independent*, p.7, 403 words, 26 February 1992.

'Doctor "Broke Guidelines" in Sex Abuse Cases: Parents say their children have been wrongly diagnosed by a consultant accused of an over-zealous approach. Families tell of humiliation and emotional scars. Rosie Waterhouse reports', *Independent*, p.4, 1,800 words, 26 September 1992.

'"Blackmail" Row over Child Abuse Inquiry', *Independent*, p.2, 600 words, 29 September 1992.

'At Breaking Point: George O'Neill had a wife, two daughters and a business. Then people started calling him a child abuser. Three times he was investigated, and three times he was cleared. And by the time they were finished with him, he had no wife, no children, and no business. His wrecked family is one of an increasing number broken by a system designed to protect children, but now abused by the malicious and malevolent', *Independent on Sunday Review*, pp.6-9, 3,000 words, 25 October 1992.

'Innocent Suffer During Inquiries into Child Abuse. Couples describe human cost of false allegations', *Independent*, 1,500 words, 1 December 1992.

'Families Urged to "Work Out" Abuse', *Independent*, 400 words, 2 December 1992.*

'Parents' Group Fights "False" Sex Abuse Claims. Solicitors are being warned about False Memory Syndrome. Rosie Waterhouse reports', *Independent*, p.2, 469 words, 11 May 1993.

'Families Haunted by Accusations of Childhood Abuse. A growing number of parents accused by adult children of ill treatment say they are victims of "false memory syndrome"', *Independent*, p.5, 1,290 words, 24 May 1993.

'Government Inquiry Decides Satanic Abuse Does Not Exist. No evidence in 84 cases of alleged black magic rituals. Evangelical Christians and self-styled 'experts' blamed for scares', *Independent on Sunday*, exclusive front page lead, 800 words, 24 April 1994.

'Rituals in Cases of Sex Abuse of Children Were "Not Satanic"', *Independent on Sunday*, p.2, 678 words, 1 May 1994.

'Abuses of Memory: What adults remember is taking over the child abuse debate. Rosie Waterhouse and Sarah Strickland report', *Independent on Sunday*, Inside Story, p.17, 2,474 words, 1 May 1994.

'Warnings on Perils of Abuse Claims', *Independent*, 400 words, 11 May 1994.

'Author of Child Sex Abuse Book is Sued', co-authored with Phil Reeves, *Independent on Sunday*, p.8, 879 words, 15 May 1994.

'Therapists Accused of Misleading Patients', *Independent*, 600 words, 1 June 1994.

Appendix 3: List of published and broadcast journalism submitted as my body of published work

'Satanic Abuse Dismissed as a "Myth" by Government Inquiry. Report blames Evangelical Christians and 'specialists' for the scare which led to investigations. Rosie Waterhouse reports', *Independent*, p.2, 784 words, 3 June 1994.

'There'll be the Devil to Pay. The future of America's 'recovered memory movement' is at stake in a $35 million lawsuit. Rosie Waterhouse reports on one family's battle', *Independent*, Life Page, p.21, 1,505 words, 17 October 1994.

'Social Workers Defy Abuse Ruling', *Independent*, p.2, 754 words, 5 March 1995.

'Crying Wolf Puts More Kids at Risk. Polemic. NSPCC claims about sex abuse are hype says Rosie Waterhouse', *Independent*, p.15, 658 words, 15 June 1995.

'So What is Child Abuse? Rosie Waterhouse reports on the latest attempts to answer a fundamental question', *Independent on Sunday*, Real Life, 1,800 words, 23 July 1995.

'New Witch Hunters. Seven years after it was completely discredited, trainee social workers are still being taught to look out for Satanic abuse', *Mail on Sunday*, p.18, 1,362 words, 1 February 1998.

'Child Abusers or Victims of Mob Justice? The *Mail on Sunday* examines why, five years after their acquittal on all charges, two nursery workers are still being accused of abusing as many as 60 toddlers. By Fiona Barton and Rosie Waterhouse', *Mail on Sunday*, pp.28-29, 2,412 words, 16 May 1999.

'Call for Inquiry into "Flawed" Report on Nursery Child Abuse', *Mail on Sunday*, p.28, 300 words, 23 May 1999. *

'Man made "false claim of abuse in care to get compensation"', *Daily Telegraph*, 800 words, 19 February 2003.

'Study casts doubt on "shaken baby syndrome"', *Daily Telegraph*, p.13, 800 words, 13 March 2003.

'Judge frees child abuse pair. Families' anger and tears over the stolen years', *Daily Telegraph*, p.14, 1800 words, 15 March 2003.

'When the mind plays tricks. Observations on sexual abuse', *New Statesman*, pp.15-16, 879 words, 15 September 2003.

'It was like a witch hunt. In October last year the remote Scottish island of Lewis was torn apart by allegations of ritual child abuse. But two weeks ago the case against the accused suddenly collapsed, just as similar actions in the Orkneys and Nottingham did before them. It was another case of 'Satanic panic', but as Rosie Waterhouse finds out, the community remains divided', *Guardian G2*, Real Lives, pp.6-7, 2,033 words, 16 July 2004.*

'Lies and a Rape of Justice. He lost his house, his job, his liberty. But though innocent, he says he will never live down the shame', *Daily Mail*, p.21, 2,000 words, 2 March 2005.

'The accusations couldn't have been more lurid. They told of devil worship, with blood being drunk as children were raped. But this week, with their lives in utter ruins, it was revealed there was not a scrap of evidence against this couple. So what on earth was going on? Special investigation by Fiona Barton and Rosie Waterhouse', *Daily Mail*, pp.38-39, 2,200 words, 15 October 2005.

'Satanic Panic: The appalling damage done to children,' *Private Eye* 1150, 20 January 2006.

Appendix 3: List of published and broadcast journalism submitted as my body of published work

'Satanic Panic: A Can of Worms', *Private Eye* 1153, 3 March 2006.

'Satanic Panic: The Mything Link', *Private Eye* 1158, 12 May 2006.

'Satanic Panic: Child Abuse', *Private Eye* 1166, 1 September 2006.

'Too Far Gonzo', *New Humanist*, book review, Blood Rites, pp36-37, 800 words, September/October, 2006.

'Locked Away on the Word of a Liar. My father was a policeman. I believed in justice. Yet I was jailed as a sex offender. Condemned by her own mother. Ruined by their anonymous accusers', *Daily Mail*, pp.8-9, 3,000 words, 13 September 2006.

'Satanic Panic: Second Opinion', *Private Eye* 1198, 23 November 2007.

'Satanic Panic: The Devil's in the Detail', *Private Eye* 1201, 11 January 2008.

'Satanic Panic: Books and Bookmen', *Private Eye* 1213, 27 June 2008.

'Weird ... or what? Why do people have paranormal experiences? A team of researchers has been trying to find out', *Guardian Education*, 1,090 words, October 14 2008.

'Satanic Panic: Meredith Kercher's murder trial part 1', *Private Eye* 1225, 12 December 2008.

'Satanic Panic: Meredith Kercher's murder trial part 2', *Private Eye* 1227, 9 January 2009

'Satanic Panic: Beatrix Potty', *Private Eye* 1240, 10 July 2009.

'Satanic Panic: It was 20 years ago today', *Private Eye* 1244, 4 September 2009.

'Satanic Panic: Justice for Carol', *Private Eye* 1302, 1,200 words, 25 November 2011.

'Satanic Panic: Devil in Disguise', *Private Eye* 1307, 600 words, 10 February 2012.

'Satanic Panic: Devil Woman', *Private Eye* 1325, 500 words, 18 October 2012.

'Satanic Panic: Familiar Ritual', *Private Eye* 1334, 800 words, 22 February 2013.

'The Woman who had 48 Personalities', *New Scientist*, 2,300 words, 28 September 2013, pp.46-49.

b. Television

BBC *Newsnight*

As reporter (see DVD):

North Wales Tribunal historic allegations of child abuse in children's homes – curtain raiser, 17 January 1997.

Colin Ross, American Dissociation 'expert', 10 February 1997.

As consultant:

Lewis case – 16 July 2004 (see entry for *Guardian*, 16 July 2004, 'It was Like a Witch Hunt').

BBC1 *Real Story*

Consultant: *The Rochdale Children*, January 11, 2006.

c. Radio

Extended interview Little Atoms March 28, 2008, http://www.littleatoms.com/waterhouse.htm, retrieved 2 December 2013.

d. Film

Advisor on authenticity of portrayal of investigative journalism, feature film *Chromophobia*, directed by Martha Fiennes, which debuted at the Cannes Festival in 2005. Screen credit.

e. Book chapter

Waterhouse, R. (2011) 'Can You Teach Investigative Journalism? Methods and Sources Old and New', in Mair, J., Keeble, R.L. (Eds) *Investigative Journalism: Dead or Alive?* Bury St. Edmunds: Abramis Academic.

f. Conference talks

British False Memory Society 12th Annual General Meeting March 25, 2006. 'From Satanic Panic to Dissociation – a media perspective.'

Centre for Investigative Journalism, Summer school, University of Westminster, July 2006. On a panel - How to avoid being conned - 'How do you investigate something that doesn't exist?'

March 2011, University of Coventry. Coventry Conversations, conference organised jointly with BBC College of Journalism – Investigative Journalism: Dead or Alive?

'Can you teach Investigative Journalism: methods and sources old and new.'

g. Presentations

October 29 2013, Goldsmiths, University of London. Anomalistic Psychology Research Unit, Invited Speakers series: Satanic Ritual Abuse, False Memories and Multiple Personalities: Anatomy of a 23 year investigation. (*see email notice from Psychology of the Paranormal Email Network 23 October 2013.)

h. Professional memberships

National Union of Journalists

The Frontline Club

Women in Journalism

Universities and Colleges Union

Associate Member of the Higher Education Academy, 2004.

Printed in Great Britain
by Amazon